GW00836613

DOM EUGENE BOYLAN

Trappist Monk, Scientist & Writer

THOMAS J MORRISSEY SJ

Published by Messenger Publications, 2019
Copyright © Thomas J Morrissey SJ, 2019

The right of Thomas J Morrissey SJ to be identified as the author of the
Work has been asserted by him in accordance with the
Copyright and Related Rights Act, 2000.

All rights reserved. No part of this book may be reproduced or utilised in any
form or by any means electronic or mechanical including photography, filming,
recording, video recording, photocopying or by any information storage and
retrieval system or shall not by way of trade or otherwise be lent, resold or
otherwise circulated in any form of binding or cover other than that in which it is
published without prior permission in writing from the publisher.

ISBN 978 1 78812 025 8

Designed by Messenger Publications Design Department
Typeset in Adobe Caslon Pro & Trajan
Printed by Hussar Books

Messenger Publications,
37 Lower Leeson Street, Dublin D02 W938
www.messenger.ie

DOM EUGENE BOYLAN, o.c.s.o.

FOURTH ABBOT

MOUNT ST. JOSEPH ABBEY, ROSCREA

Born	February 3rd 1904
Entered Monastery	September 8th 1931
Received Habit	October 11th 1931
Solemn Vows	October 15th 1936
Ordained Priest	May 9th 1937
Australian Foundation	1953-1955
Superior Caldey Abbey	1955-1959
Elected Abbot, Roscrea	July 11th 1962
Abbatial Blessing	August 5th 1962
Died	January 5th 1964

DOM EUGENE BOYLAN

CONTENTS

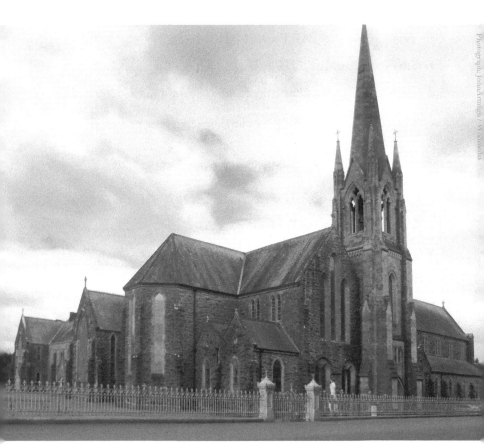

Mount St Joseph Abbey, Roscrea

Photograph: JohnArmagh / Wikimedia

ACKNOWLEDGEMENTS

This book owes its existence to the former abbot of Mount St Joseph Abbey, Roscrea, and now Abbot of Mount Melleray, Dom Richard Purcell. He made it possible for me to stay at the monastery, explore the archives, and experience the life and kindness of the monks. In addition, Fr Laurence Walsh, author and archivist, was a constant source of advice and necessary information throughout the research and writing of this work.

As a reading of the book makes evident, very much assistance came from the research of the late Fr Nivard Kinsella, who compiled much information from family and contemporaries of Eugene Boylan. I have also received help in preparing the book from the work done by Dr Louise O'Reilly in the monastery archives and in relation to Abbot Boylan. For background material I have been fortunate to be able to call on the resource of Milltown Park Library and its most efficient and accommodating staff, June, Àine and Anne.

This form of spiritual biography is a new genre of biography for me, so I am greatly indebted to two readers of the text: Fr Laurence Walsh, above, who assured me of the general accuracy of the book in relation to monastic life and Eugene Boylan, and to a fellow Jesuit, Dr Brian O'Leary, an esteemed writer in the field of spirituality. Finally, my thanks and appreciation to my provincial, Fr Leonard Moloney, for his on-going interest and encouragement, and to my community at Milltown Park for their patience and support.

Thomas J Morrissey SJ

Richard and Agnes Boylan. Caption on the back of the photograph reads: Our beloved parents; Richard, died 17 Sept 1939. Agnes, 11th May 1961. RIP.

PART ONE: 1904–29

Agnes Boylan with baby Kevin. Caption on the back reads: 'In the nursery'.

CHAPTER 1

HOME AND SCHOOL YEARS, 1904–21

In the seaside town of Bray, Co. Wicklow, some twenty kilometres from Dublin city, Eugene Boylan was born on 3 February 1904. The first child of Richard and Agnes (née Colclough) Boylan, he weighed, as he later proudly related, a sturdy 12 lbs 12 ozs at birth.[1] Eugene – the name he adopted on entering monastic life – was baptised Richard Kevin, but was generally known as Kevin to his family and friends to distinguish him from his father. His sister Mary – known as Molly – was born the following year, and his brother Dermot in 1906.

---

1   Eugene Boylan's manuscript account of his early years, Mount St Joseph's Archives (MSJA), 5/5/3, no.1, Mount St Joseph Abbey, Roscrea.

Agnes Boylan.

FIRST YEARS IN BRAY AND KELLS

Richard Boylan, a quiet, thoughtful and well-read man, was sub-manager of the Hibernian Bank in Bray. Agnes, a tall, handsome woman of commanding presence, was outgoing and vivacious. She delighted in company and was frequently the centre of the party. As a gifted musician with a good voice, she loved to draw people to her house for musical evenings. She was in charge of the Pro-Cathedral's Palestrina Choir under the aegis of Dr Nicholas Donnelly, Auxiliary Bishop of Dublin, as well as organist at the local Catholic church.[2] Agnes was the youngest of fourteen children. Her mother, who lived with the Boylan family, played a major part in rearing the children.

2   Eugene Boylan's typed manuscript account of his early years, MSJA.

Kevin Boylan had happy memories of his early years, and these memories were later supplemented by what others told him. In this way he learned how, on one occasion, when his mother hosted a dinner party for the local clergy at her house, he had taken the coffee pot from the kitchen and was happily pouring the contents down the sink. When his deed was detected, his reply – 'I'll do it my 'elf' – was not without significance in view of his later career. It was a frequent protest of his.[3]

When Kevin was three years old, his father was appointed bank manager in the market town of Kells in Co. Meath, to where the family moved in 1907, and where a year later, a third son, Gerald, was born. They lived in the big bank house in the town; it had a large garden, but they missed the sea. Kevin's memories from that time were of the garden and of music in the house. His grandmother presided over a large room called the nursery, where all the children, except the baby, slept. Kevin's great friend was his father. They went for walks together, and until the end of his life he remembered them walking together in a wood in Headfort Estate near Kells. To be like his father he gave up taking sugar in his tea.

They were only eighteen months in Kells when Richard was appointed to the Dublin area as an inspector, and the family found themselves on the move again. At this point, they rented a house in Monkstown, Co. Dublin, quite near the town of Kingstown – now Dún Laoghaire.

HAPPY YEARS IN MONKSTOWN

'For the next four years,' Kevin recalled, 'we lived at 4 Trafalgar Terrace, opposite to Seapoint Tower. Those were halcyon years. The sea was at our door'. Not surprisingly, it was there that he learned to swim. He remembered that his father was away for most of the week and that his mother played a lot of Bridge. There was also 'a fair share of music' in the house. 'My grandmother's big room was the nursery', he remembered. 'She made most of our clothes, told us stories and later made us read to her. She had a lot to do with our

3   Eugene Boylan's typed manuscript account of his early years, MSJA.

mental development.' One story she told had a snake in it, and this, Kevin surmised, might explain his later almost pathological fear and loathing of snakes. 'Those evenings when my father came home were memorable … I can't ever remember being beaten, or any one of the three – father, mother, grandmother – having any difficulty in controlling us, although we were mischievous enough. I don't think we were unduly subdued, our submission was through love rather than fear.'

A second daughter, Kathleen, was born in 1910, bringing the number of children to five. All of them seem to have had equally happy memories of home, to judge by the passing references they made to their childhood and to the great regard in which they held their parents. Theirs was a quietly religious home without undue piety.

When he was five years old, Kevin and his sister, Molly, were sent to school by tram to the Dominican Convent school in Kingstown. Kevin had few memories of his time there, although he did recall walking home with another boy by the seashore. In the school, he and a French boy were soon moved up to senior school, where they were the only boys among the girls. He remembered himself and the other boy walking round and round the square at recreation, the two of them remaining at the back. He also remembered trying to learn spelling and French, without much success, and he recalled a childish prank that didn't quite come off. 'I remember putting back the clock in school to prolong the recreation, but the nun's watch decided matters.'

Kevin recalled a few children's parties from those years. At one of these, Postman's Knock was played, which involved the loser having to kiss another player. He refused to play. On the other hand, at a pantomime for his seventh birthday he fell in love with the principal 'boy'. Subsequently, he recalled, 'I looked for her at Mass every Sunday in Monkstown church'. Kevin added, 'I liked going to Mass with my parents, but I was by no means religious or devout'.

On a similar revelatory note, he commented that he was sensitive about the home-made clothes he wore, and that he hated having to share a bed with his brother, Dermot. As he watched Dermot, who was obviously more athletic, climb from one tree to another, he made excuses for not attempting the same feat himself, admitting that 'I was always timid about such things, somewhat of a physical coward'. His final comment on his years in Monkstown bespoke the hard-won experience of an eight-year-old: 'I always dreaded going with my mother in trams etc. She talked out loud about what I felt were my own personal matters – with herself and my grandmother. Although there was great love and unlimited kindness, one knew it was impossible to sway them from their purpose.'

In 1912, Richard Boylan was appointed manager of the Hibernian Bank in Derry, and the family had to uproot itself again. They were to live there for the next twelve years.

THE MOVE TO DERRY

Life in the northern city was in many ways a new experience. Derry, they found, was largely dominated by antagonism between the Protestant and Catholic communities. A few years after the Boylans' arrival, the First World War broke out, followed by the Irish Revolution and the subsequent War of Independence. As a result, the inbuilt antagonism in Derry took on additional bitterness and aggression, particularly after 1918. Nevertheless, the Boylan children grew up in an atmosphere remarkably free of sectarianism, bigotry and political zealotry.

The reason for this can be largely attributed to their father. He was the only Catholic bank manager in Derry, while all of his professional colleagues, many of whom visited the house, were Protestants. Richard Boylan was politically a home ruler in sympathy, and was opposed to violence. He was highly respected in the banking profession, and had a quiet ease of manner and a sense of humour that disarmed any opposition. His sons recalled him teasing his colleagues about their strong anti-gambling tenets as Presbyterians, while pleading with them to play bridge for 'a halfpenny a hundred'. As a consequence of these good relations, the children experienced no intrinsic antagonism because they came from Dublin, and they accepted friendship with Protestants as a normal part of life.

Richard's manifest integrity and openness, and his position as a Catholic bank manager, also led to his being highly regarded by the Catholic professional community. This was reinforced by his wife's hospitality and talents. Her musical gifts and reputation led to requests for her to train school choirs, and the hospitable Boylan House became a meeting place for Catholic professional men, and especially for the Catholic clergy. Evenings were frequently enlivened by gatherings around the family piano.[4]

Kevin's memory on his arrival in Derry was of a large bank house with a tiny yard. It was situated on a street corner, and there was no garden, no grass, no sea and no place to play. 'When on my own, I spent all my time down on the quays watching the ships and longing for a boat of my own.' For his education he was sent to a local convent school, which catered for young boys and girls, but he did not enjoy his time there. After a year or so, he transferred to the Christian Brothers' primary school at 'the Brow of the Hill'. There, as he recalled, 'there was hardly anyone of my own "class". Well-to-do Catholics were few and far between in Derry. My sister's first comment, when we came later to Dublin, was on the number of well-dressed people at Mass.'[5]

'In Derry,' Kevin added, 'I became conscious of the fact that I was the son of "Somebody". My father was considered one of the leading citizens. My mother's personality, music and bridge put her in the forefront. My grandmother never left the top storey, and never saw our visitors save a few.' Nevertheless, Kevin remembered about his grandmother that 'she had a clear grasp of everyone we knew in Derry, their history, their relations etc. She had an amazing mind. She taught us to play chess, made us read the news for her, discussed politics with us, and kept us up to the mark mentally.'

Kevin always retained fond memories of his father. 'My father had extraordinary general knowledge. He was a misfit in the bank,

4   Eugene Boylan's typed manuscript account of his early years, p. 3, MSJA.
5   Eugene Boylan's typed manuscript account of his early years, MSJA.

although he was then considered one of their best men. He was not a "pusher" nor did he keep his goods in the shop window. He was one of the most popular men in Derry.' For the children 'home was always our favourite place', and for Kevin as a ten-year-old 'to go somewhere with my father was one of my greatest pleasures'.

FAMILY LIFE IN DERRY

Kevin's sister, Kathleen, provided an insight into her brother's personality during those years in Derry. 'He was very inquisitive as a child,' she said, 'always asking questions. He was forever taking his toys apart to see how they worked. He liked jigsaw puzzles and mechanical games.' He obviously took seriously his responsibility as the eldest child. 'He was always the "big brother" to the rest of us, and on family outings and on special occasions he liked to settle everything and us so that there would be no hitch. On the occasion of a family photograph, he fussed so much placing his brothers and sisters that the exasperated photographer queried, "Young man, are you taking this photograph or am I?"'

Kathleen also provided a revealing family vignette, when she recalled that Kevin 'was inclined to be hot-tempered and over a trifling thing sometimes, but he would cool down as quickly as he had boiled up and would try to make up by being extra nice afterwards. My brothers used to delight in teasing him on this account, and they would hide his belongings – his boots or tie – on First Friday mornings when they were rushing out to Mass.[6] The resulting scene was hardly a fitting preparation, but no doubt his acts of sorrow and love were all the more fervent by way of making up.'

Kathleen also recalled that Kevin, having developed a desire to go to daily Mass and communion, used to ask her to call him in time for the eight o'clock Mass. It didn't prove to be easy, however. Kevin worked late at night and was difficult to wake up. 'Pulling and hauling and even cold water might get one eye open and a grunt, but it would shut at once and off again'. 'We missed him very much,' she

6   Devotion to the Sacred Heart of Jesus was frequently marked by attendance at Mass on the first Friday in each month. The Boylan family clearly participated in this devotion.

15

added, 'when he went to Dublin about the age of fourteen.'[7]

The Boylan children seem to have kept to themselves a good deal, having their own games and musical performances. Kevin had a lot of energy, some of which he expended on cycling. It is mentioned that he cycled around the walls of Derry with his sister on the crossbar! There were times, however, when his experience with boys less well-off than himself was less than pleasant. In retrospect, he made this frank disclosure: 'I was not a "fighter" and made an ass of myself in a few quarrels. More than once I came home with a bloody nose. I generally gave in, crying, once that started.' Despite his poor performance in these fights and his more privileged background, he was not ridiculed as a 'sissy', and was somehow respected by his peers.

Music and singing came easily to him. 'I was found to have a voice and (was) put in the Cathedral Choir. Later on, I was ambitious to sing solo (in the Derry Feis or musical festival), but there was one boy with a better voice.' Kevin was defeated by this boy in the competition, but only by one mark. His treble voice meant that he could partake with all the rest of the family 'in scenes from grand opera' which 'were got up at home'.[8] His mother tried to teach him the piano, but without success. 'I could never learn anything from her,' he later admitted. 'My father was the only authority acceptable in things intellectual. It was he who showed me how to finger a scale. I gradually learned to read music, but never "practised".'

When he was eleven or twelve years old, he 'got a year's lessons from Joe O'Brien,' and 'to my amazement won the Junior Piano in the Derry Feis'. According to the version of this story told by Kathleen, he may not have been all that surprised by his victory. She recalled that on the day of the competition at the Guildhall, his mother found him with other boys sliding up and down the shining wide corridors instead of quietly relaxing as he waited for his turn to play. When she accosted him, he reassured her with the reply, 'Oh, I can do as well as any of them, I needn't worry'. His

---

7   Magdalen Boylan to Fr Nivard, 'A Few Memories About Eugene', MSJA. Magdalen was Kathleen's name in religion.
8   Magdalen to Fr Nivard, MSJA.

sister added, 'He was always singularly free from conceit about his achievements, musical or otherwise, but he knew what he could do.'[9] His open expression of confidence would not infrequently lead to misunderstanding. Socially, he displayed a mixture of confidence, distance, naïvety and, at times, insensitivity.

LIFE AT SCHOOL IN DERRY
Kevin provided much information about his years spent in Derry. At the Christian Brothers' primary school he began to shine, especially at mathematics. 'But', he admitted, 'I could never learn things by rote. Catechism class was a torture, especially with one brother, who believed in the leather as a mnemonic.' Because the brothers were not in a position to prepare pupils for the intermediate system, they focused on science and technical subjects. No languages were taught, except a little Irish. 'I was happy there at school', Kevin reflected, 'except where we had a master who believed in the "leather". This used paralyse me.'

The school did not have any games or sports days, which did not greatly disappoint Kevin. 'I was hopelessly awkward on the field,' he later recalled. It had the effect, however, of helping him to discover 'the glamour of books'. 'I read fiction omnivorously – boys' stories, also books about machines, etc.' As his sister intimated, he was full of questions in the classroom. The brother teaching him complained in frustration that an encyclopaedia would be necessary to answer all of them. 'I was very "gullible",' Kevin admitted, 'and in some ways very simple, but I had a reasoning mind and was always working out "whys" and looking for new ways of doing things. Science was my great attraction. I wanted to be an "inventor".'

HOLIDAYS BY THE SEA
Summer holidays from Derry were spent in a farmhouse near Magilligan Strand, a long stretch on the northern coastline of Co. Derry. It was a quiet area, lacking the crowds and excitement of seaside resorts. There was a post office, a small number of houses, and

9   Magdalen to Fr Nivard, MSJA.

seven long miles of sand and dunes. Kevin loved the sea, although he bemoaned the absence of smooth water for those learning to swim, and the lack of pools for fishing. The family greatly enjoyed themselves on these occasions and, as might be expected, Kevin's enjoyment was linked to his father being with them. 'We could never really enjoy a walk or a bathe unless we got my father to come with us. I remember being intensely jealous when he and my younger brother went off alone. I was very strong in my "rights" as the eldest son and took my pre-eminence for granted.' Looking back across the years, Kevin recalled only sunny days. 'After our bathes we used to lie in the sun for hours. Until twenty-five years of age I counted a summer day wasted that I did not get a bathe.'

AT O'CONNELL SCHOOL IN DUBLIN

In 1917, when Kevin was approaching fourteen years of age, it was decided to send him to Dublin to start his intermediate education. His father had himself attended O'Connell School in North Richmond St, Dublin, and had a high opinion of the education provided by the Christian Brothers. Kevin was enrolled there. This was made possible by the fact that he was able to stay in Dublin with his aunt – his mother's sister – and her husband. They were both teachers, had no children, and were reasonably well off. In time they also accepted Kevin's brother, Dermot, into their home. They lived in a small house in Charleville Road, Rathmines, a suburb some distance across the city from Richmond St. This meant that Kevin had to cycle to and from school each day. Conscious of the tight finances at home, and encouraged to study hard by his parents, and especially wishing to please his father, he determined to do well in his new school. Already he had the ability to take in at a glance what he read, which gave him the edge over many of the others in intellectual pursuits.

At his new school, it soon became clear that Kevin related easily to older people. According to a former classmate of his, Donal Flood, in an interview with Fr Nivard of Roscrea, Kevin became popular among the Christian Brothers, especially the influential Br Galvin, who was known among the boys as 'the Guvner'.[10] Br Galvin, who was in charge of the honours students and a very good teacher, took to Kevin and brought him into his class. As the emphasis was on maths and science, Kevin soon felt at home.[11] Kevin also developed a special relationship with one other teacher, a Mr Patrick Kennedy, who taught English.

Flood described Kevin as not mixing much with the other boys and having just 'a superficial contact with everyone', although he was 'a very lively and likeable type'. He noted that Kevin's travelling to and from school took up much time, and he believed that this partly explained why he did not have friends among his peers. On the other hand, as Flood noted, Kevin found time to seek out older people, especially those with influence. Flood – whose mother, like Kevin's, was a music teacher and who had her views on Mrs Boylan – attributed this characteristic to the influence of Kevin's mother. Flood also intimated that Kevin had 'the same type of character' as Br Galvin, who 'always made for the important people, and knew all the important people.'[12]

Br Galvin was a more significant figure than Flood acknowledged. He was an outstanding educator, who saw the potentialities of young people like Kevin and encouraged them to greater efforts. He was an unusual man in many ways. Something of an imperialist in his politics, he favoured home rule within the empire, wishing to achieve it by peaceful political methods rather than by the means espoused by the physical force movement. Since this stance coincided with that of Kevin's father, who was a follower of John Redmond and the Irish Parliamentary Party, and since it also agreed with his own temperamental inclination, Kevin absorbed these ideas and carried them into his adult life.

The other teacher who greatly influenced him, Mr Kennedy, was also a devoted educationalist. Gifted not only with a talent for teaching English, he also had a wide knowledge of music and, in

10 D. Flood interviewed by Fr Nivard, 17 November 1964, MSJA. From the school records, it is clear that the 'D' stood for Donal.
11 Eugene Boylan's typed manuscript account of his early years, MSJA.
12 Flood interviewed by Fr Nivard, MSJA.

addition, was a classical scholar of some distinction. He edited a number of school texts of the Latin classics and imparted such an appreciation of them to Kevin that years later, as a monk, he would read Livy and Caesar for pleasure.[13]

Kevin did well at school. In the summer of 1918 he sat for his Junior Grade examination and passed it with a prize. He was to repeat this success right through his subsequent years in school and university, so that he succeeded, more or less, in paying all his fees by means of scholarships and prizes. The following year he took his Middle Grade examination, and this time won a money prize worth £3, and also a medal for gaining full marks in Algebra. Interestingly, while he took honours in his mathematical and science subjects, he merely passed in languages.

That year was the year of the great influenza epidemic in the wake of the First World War. Thousands died in Ireland, and schools closed for several weeks. Kevin, however, escaped the infection, and he used the unexpected free time for further reading and more swimming. By this time, he had been joined in Rathmines by his brother Dermot. Like Kevin, Dermot showed considerable intellectual ability, but was less of an individualist.

The following year, being younger than many of his classmates, Kevin stayed on in Middle Grade on the advice of Br Galvin, hoping to gain an Exhibition. He achieved his aim. He got first place in mathematics, and second in science, and received an Exhibition worth £20, which more than covered his school fees. His marks throughout his time at school were consistent, scoring high in mathematics and science, but with an invariable pass in languages. This last contrasts strangely with the flair for languages he later showed.

During his final year at school a small incident occurred which profoundly impressed him, and about which he often spoke later. His English teacher, the Mr Kennedy previously mentioned, set the class an essay entitled 'What I would like to be'. When the essays were being returned to the boys, the teacher remarked, 'I

13 Typed document entitled 'Chapter I', p. 7, MSJA. Presumably part of Fr Nivard's projected work on Eugene Boylan.

am surprised that out of a class of Catholic boys, not one of you said that he wanted to become a saint'. This remark, made perhaps spontaneously and without any further comment, had a singular effect on Kevin. He never forgot it, often repeating the remark in later years and implying that he owed his seriousness about his religion to it.[14] To the end of his life, he considered himself in debt to this remarkable teacher and friend.

In that final year, Kevin had an ambitious academic programme in mind, hoping to win a scholarship in order to continue his studies at university level. He was also faced with a decision about entering a seminary, however. He sought the advice of a Jesuit confessor about a vocation to the priesthood,[15] and the counsel he received appears to have been encouraging. By now, Br Galvin had moved elsewhere, but the brother in charge of Kevin's class was aware of his dilemma. He advised Kevin to work hard for the scholarship; then, bolstered by the scholarship, to seek permission in the seminary to do mathematics and science at the university, where the seminary students studied for their degrees.

Kevin was duly entered for the scholarship examination of the Royal College of Science, taking second place and gaining a scholarship worth £75 a year for four years. At the same time, he took the normal Senior Grade examination and gained two £30 exhibitions. He was also awarded medals for mathematics and science by the school.[16]

LIFE OUTSIDE SCHOOL

During his years in Dublin, Kevin, as will later appear, developed a mixed range of activities. He enthusiastically continued his interest in music. 'I used to go to the Gaiety every Saturday night (top gallery). I never missed an opera or a celebrity concert.' He used to meet his English teacher, Mr Kennedy, at the opera or at a Gilbert and Sullivan performance. 'He', Kevin admitted, 'had

---

14 Typed manuscript entitled 'Chapter I', pp. 9–10, MSJA.
15 Typed manuscript entitled, 'Chapter I', MSJA.
16 Typed manuscript entitled, 'Chapter I', MSJA.

a lot to do with my musical education.'[17]

In Rathmines, Kevin acquired a ticket to the Carnegie Library. 'I read one book of fiction every night', he later recalled. His other reading was of works of a mechanical or scientific interest. On Sundays he used to go back to Monkstown and Kingstown 'for old times' sake', and before long he discovered the Blackrock Baths. 'I had learned to swim and there I developed "a style".' Swimming made a great difference to his life. He took part in training sessions and in competitions, and proved successful in a number of events. Even in winter, he continued to swim at the Iveagh Baths in the city centre. His sister, Kathleen, remembered that 'he won a good few races, had a very graceful style, and later represented Ireland in the Tailteann Games'.[18]

In those years he naturally became interested in girls. He read romantic fiction with happy endings, and developed a romantic outlook himself. He had one unattainable girl in mind, but had confused views about sex. 'I began to long for a girlfriend,' he revealed, 'but I never had the courage to make advances. I had no contact with girls of my own age.' On one occasion in the Religious Instruction class, the brother in charge asked them to write down questions they would wish to ask. The questions posed in Kevin's case were such that 'the brother took me apart and gave me a fair amount of enlightenment. This was a relief to me as I had been of a general desire to be good and to choose a way of life that would lead to "success" in the next world.'

He was very lonely at times during his first couple of years in Dublin before Dermot arrived, and looked forward to returning to Derry three times each year. The welcoming and affectionate atmosphere at home, joined to the devoted religious practice of his parents and the frequent visits of clergy to the house, all encouraged an interest in a formal religious way of life and raised the question of a possible vocation.

---

17 Eugene Boylan's typed manuscript account of his early years, MSJA.
18 Eugene Boylan's typed manuscript account of his early years, MSJA. The Tailteann Games ran from 1924–1932.

Kevin's younger sister, Kathleen, joined the Cistercian nuns at Glencairn, Co. Waterford, where she was known as Sr Magdalen. Kevin's other sister, Molly (above), entered the Congregation of Marie Reparatrice in the United States.

Kevin was not the only one in the family to experience similar desires and to act on them. His brother, Dermot, would be ordained a priest in the Dublin diocese and subsequently would enter Parkminster Charterhouse, the Carthusian monastery in England, from where he would be sent to a new Carthusian foundation in the United States of America. He was known in religion as Fr Stephen Boylan. Kevin's younger sister, Kathleen, joined the Cistercian nuns at Glencairn, Co. Waterford, where she was known as Sr Magdalen. Kevin's other sister, Molly, entered the Congregation of Marie

Reparatrice in the United States. The final member of the family, Gerald, married and had a family of his own. Kevin maintained a close relationship with each of his sisters and brothers.

A SELF-CONFIDENT YOUNG MAN

Kevin Boylan left O'Connell School loaded with academic honours. He was conscious of his achievements and quietly proud of them. Tending to be a loner, he had a degree of self-confidence perhaps unusual for someone his age, mixing more easily with chosen adult company than with other boys. This trait was noted by his contemporaries, as was his academic competence, but did not lead to dissension or any notable absence of popularity. This may well have been due to the high academic standards promoted by the school. There were other boys in the school who were Boylan's equals academically. The prize lists of the years Eugene spent in O'Connell School tell of a group of young students who were consistently well placed in examinations, taking numerous prizes and scholarships, and who then repeated the pattern at university. At one level, Kevin was unaware of his own superiority among his peers, and tended to treat others as his intellectual equals. Hence, the 'humility' to which his sister referred. He was friendly to all in a rather superficial manner, but was close to few – and these were adults. He was influenced by them because he admired them.

At this point, as he concluded his years at secondary school, it is interesting to note that although Kevin attended school in Dublin during the years of the Irish War of Independence, 1918–21, there is no extant reference in his papers to the politics and violent events of those years. His recollections of his schooldays, written in his later years, are of an apparently undisturbed, normal way of life. If his feelings were touched by some of the sad and poignant events in those years, as they must surely have been, no record of them remains.

CHAPTER 2

CLONLIFFE COLLEGE AND UNIVERSITY COLLEGE DUBLIN, 1921–26

In September 1921 Kevin began training for the priesthood. Because he was more impressed by Dublin clergy than by those he met in Derry, and also because his father favoured Dublin and planned to retire there, Kevin applied for entry to Holy Cross College, Clonliffe, the seminary for the Dublin Archdiocese. He entered on 30 September 1921, and started his studies in University College Dublin shortly afterwards.[19] From the authorities in Clonliffe College he obtained permission to study mathematics and science, as he had hoped. His situation was quite unusual, since it involved attending practical classes at times different from those of other Clonliffe students. The result was that 'I was doing lectures by myself except for Latin, Irish and English'. He worked hard and made no attempt to hide his ambition to achieve honours. This was not appreciated by many of his fellow seminarians, who seemed determined to do the minimum amount of work and to be satisfied with a pass degree.

UNHAPPY MEMORIES OF CLONLIFFE

In his later recollection as a monk, Kevin observed, with some exaggeration, that 'Clonliffe was torture from the beginning'. Certainly, in retrospect, features of seminary life repelled him, but at first he seemed to find outlets which made life interesting. 'I cannot say I was unpopular,' Kevin admitted, 'but I got many a covert dig that would have been all the easier to handle had it been more open … The fact that I took honours lectures was a very black mark against me.'

He went on to imply that the fault was partly his own. 'I remember going out for the First Year Physics examination and

19 Letter of the President of Holy Cross College, Clonliffe to Fr Nivard, 9 April 1965, MSJA.

being asked how I thought I'd do. "Well," I said, "I should manage honours and, with a bit of luck, it might be a first class". This created endless comment ... When next year I went on to do an honours degree in physics I was a marked man.' At the same time, Kevin had to admit, 'It should, of course, have been fairly easy to live down all that and laugh it off, but I couldn't control either my voice or my features, and often when the remarks were not addressed to me – my reaction did not improve matters.' He quoted a priest friend saying to him in later years that at that time he, Kevin, 'was full of pride'.

His home life and the years living largely on his own in Dublin had not been a good preparation for seminary life. His father's way of dealing with his children was to put them on trust, and to expect them to act responsibly in an environment in which they were loved. It was successful. As a result, the constant supervision involved in seminary life was irksome, as were the inbuilt restraints against individual expression. 'In the college,' he observed, 'each had a room, but after dinner, from about 3.00–5.00pm, we had recreation and were not allowed return to our rooms. Some tried to play soccer, but having to play in their gowns only a few persevered. That left a walk around the grounds with a companion. You were obliged to go with the first group you met and take your place there in ascending seniority. The same held for the evening recreation, 8.30–9.00pm. This was almost unbearable. Frequently I was with a group where I knew I wasn't wanted, was butting in on old friends. Given my hypersensitivity, I felt ill at ease where it was not justified. At best I talked foolishly, but when under tension, it was twice as bad.'

The seminary regimentation extended to walking to the university: 'One had to walk in twos with an appointed partner, who was changed three or four times a year'. (It did not seem to occur to Kevin that the intention behind this practice was to avoid cliques or exclusive friendships among the students.) Perhaps most difficult of all was the prefect system, which seemed geared to finding fault. It was out of kilter with his father's way of acting. In addition to all these negative factors, as he recorded them in later life, he found the staff of the college remote, reserved, and 'untouchable'. He recalled that 'I had one friend on the staff, a priest, who was a schoolfellow of my father, was a "students' man" and a continual thorn in the side of the authorities. Only for him, life would have been impossible.' Revealingly, Kevin commented, 'It was in Clonliffe that I first found myself not quite "so approved of" by the authorities … An uncle as parish priest was a far better recommendation than a scholastic record.'

THE RECOLLECTIONS OF OTHERS

Memory can be remarkably selective. The dark picture that remained in Kevin's mind had, in reality, a good deal of colour to it. For one thing, he had acquired a nickname, suggesting a certain ease with other students. The Boylan family tended to be rather formal in their relationships. They addressed others as Father, Mister, Miss, etc., and they seldom used Christian names. Men tended to use their surnames in addressing each other, and nicknames would have been considered in poor taste. Already in O'Connell School, however, Kevin had been given a nickname, based on his tendency to sign himself R. K. Boylan. He became known 'Orky'.[20] Then at Clonliffe he was given another nickname, where he became known as 'Dicky' Boylan to his fellow students. It was Robert Nash, in preparing a long article on Eugene Boylan, who learned, among other things, of Kevin's nickname, after meeting some of Kevin's former contemporaries at Clonliffe.[21]

Some other recollections revealed to Nash indicated that during his youth Kevin had been engaged in unexpectedly non-academic activities. Thus, in Clonliffe he was remembered as having a considerable knowledge of horses: their breeding, their racing form and the likely outcome of a race in which a particular horse was involved. He took into account the nature of the different race courses – a left-hand course or a right-hand one, an uphill finish – and how these suited different horses. His memory was said

20 Nivard Kinsella, pamphlet, *Dom Eugene Boylan (1904–1963)*, p. 1.
21 Robert Nash SJ, 'Dom Eugene Boylan (1903–1963, Cistercian, Monk and Abbot)' in *Ten More Priests* (Dublin: Clanmore & Reynolds Ltd, 1965), p. 19.

to be prodigious on such matters. It seems likely that he frequented some of Dublin's racecourses at Baldoyle, Leopardstown and the Phoenix Park.

Swimming, as noted earlier was his special sport, and once again his memory was remarkable, being able to recall the times and distances of swimmers over the years. As regards other interests, he was remembered as enjoying the debating society and the spirited arguments that would sometimes carry over into private conversation. He also enjoyed a clever epigram, a pointed anecdote and a good story. He had definite political views on Irish affairs, it seems, but was reluctant to air them, probably because the tension and bitterness of the civil war discouraged discussion of these matters. On political issues abroad, however, he expressed his views more readily. He believed that the Peace of Versailles was the work of Freemasons, that it was unjust and could not last. In those days, when the map of Europe was being virtually redrawn, he was strongly of the opinion, that Catholic Germany – Austria, Bavaria and the Rhineland – should be united in one state to balance the militarism of the Junkers, the exclusive aristocratic party in Prussia.

As regards his behaviour while in Clonliffe, Kevin claimed that he kept the rules. Some of his contemporaries qualified that statement, however, recalling that he saw no harm in bypassing unnecessary and repressive regulations. They remembered, as mentioned earlier, that he despised the prefect system, which kept the students under observation and checked for their transgressions. Reflecting his father's attitude, he argued that the students should be treated as adults, and that such supervision developed a sneaky, subservient spirit that contributed little to the formation of a priestly character. He disliked the subterfuges by which some other students would try to extricate themselves from blame. He would always own up without excuse or palliation, and take whatever punishment was coming.[22]

In his usual frank manner, Kevin made no secret of the fact that there were financial difficulties in his family, and that it was essential

22   Nash, 'Dom Eugene Boylan' in *Ten More Priests*, p. 19.

for him to win scholarships if he was to continue in college. It was not until his final year in O'Connell School or his first year in Clonliffe that he became aware of how fraught the family finances really were. His father was a prudent, patient man, but his mother was extravagant with their money, not by spending it on herself directly, but in her role as hostess for evenings of music, entertainment and dining, when she was the pleasantly dominant focus of attention. Kevin loved his mother, and took after her in many ways, but he was not blind to her failings and to the financial problems they raised for his father and for the children's future.

While in Clonliffe, Kevin kept up his interest in music, although opportunities for attending concerts or operas were greatly restricted. Shortage of money meant that he had to resort to a savings programme in order to attend a celebrity concert. He invented pretexts, such as an urgent appointment with a dentist, to get from the college to a concert. On one occasion, the dean saw through one of these excuses and, not being amused, he confined Kevin to the college. It was said that Kevin frequently examined with longing the catalogues of gramophone records, the prices of which were beyond him.

Once again, in contrast to Kevin's stark depiction of his life at Clonliffe, the contemporaries whom Nash met remembered him as well liked, being entertaining and amusing in conversation. He was usually in good humour, they recalled, was transparently honest, not ostensibly pious, a good mixer, a good student, well informed on contemporary questions and able to talk about them intelligently. One must conclude that while Kevin's memory of his years in Clonliffe had darkened over the years, his contemporaries, looking back on someone who had since become famous, may have viewed his time in Clonliffe in a more positive light than was merited. The truth, we can assume, lies somewhere in between.

AN UNUSUAL CLERICAL STUDENT

Donal Flood, who had been friendly with Kevin when they were in the same class in O'Connell School, had gone ahead of him when

Kevin stayed back to repeat the Intermediate examination. They met again at university, where they both studied science. Donal clearly found Kevin quite unusual as a clerical student. 'He didn't tend to cling to the other "black coats", as we used to call them. You would find him roaming around the college and mixing with everybody … When he went back to Derry on holidays he used to go to dances. At the time we used to have these private dances in people's houses … and he was always at them, which rather surprised me. I am a rather different type since if I assumed clerical garb, I imagine I would assume all the conventions that go with it. But Kevin in fact was unconventional, there is no doubt about that. He was highly individualistic. He inherited a lot of the mother's traits. I never met the mother. I only know of her because my mother often spoke about her.'[23]

Had Flood read Boylan's own account of his unconventional activities, he would really have been taken aback. 'In my years in Clonliffe,' Kevin recalled, 'the Christmas holidays were rather gay. Typically, I got as far away as I could from "clericals" on holidays, wearing grey etc. I went to any dances I could and joined in all the fun that was going. After I had been a year at Clonliffe, we spent holidays in Greencastle (Co. Donegal). There, principally through an unusual spirit of daring, I started an "affair" with a girl and we got rather fond of one another. I had no intention of marriage and had anybody suggested (it) I should have been amazed at being taken so seriously. I was then eighteen and a half. This affair lasted by letter until the Christmas holidays. During that (time) it was quite "active", but some way or another I got out of it. I felt rather mean about it. The girl afterwards got engaged to some solicitor, but was found dead in her room. There was talk of suicide and I felt very "disconcerted". Were it not for that affair, I should probably have left Clonliffe earlier.'[24]

---

23 Flood interviewed by Fr. Nivard, MSJA.
24 The incident displays Kevin's self-centredness at the time. As regards the 'affair', the consensus among those who knew Kevin Boylan was that it would not have progressed beyond a romantic stage.

LEAVING CLONLIFFE

Kevin's unhappiness in Clonliffe had to be faced eventually, however. The second year in Clonliffe, I began to get some insight into diocesan life, the need to conform to a pattern etc., and I could not see myself fitting into it at all. I thought of trying an American diocese, but was talked out of it. Finally, just before the Christmas holidays in my third year, I approached my priest friend, who was no longer on the staff. I told him how I felt, and that I found myself beginning to rebel against the whole establishment in Clonliffe. He told me in God's name to get out, and so I did with a light heart. I had prayed a good deal to be prevented from making a mistake.

About this time, Flood remembered Kevin telling him that he was going to leave Clonliffe and was thinking 'of a more serious type of life'. Flood did not believe him about his future plans, but the words remained with him and surfaced later when he heard that Kevin had joined the Cistercian monastery at Roscrea. At the time it seemed a most unlikely prospect, but an entry in Kevin's written recollection of those years suggests that he had such a possibility in mind. In conversation with his priest friend, he suggested that 'some place like Roscrea was really the place for me'. The response was firm: 'Put it out of you mind. You have neither the health nor the temperament for it' – a view with which most of his acquaintances, and at least some of his family, would concur.

Meantime, Kevin was faced with the task of informing his parents during the Christmas period that he would not be returning to Clonliffe. His sister Kathleen thought it was one of the hardest things he ever had to do. 'I remember him standing there while mother was telling me, shifting from one foot to another and looking as if he were going to cry'.[25] As it happened, it was an unpropitious time to break the news to his parents. His mother, who had been extravagant with expenditure, 'had also borrowed money very rashly. The result was that creditors began to press, and my

25 Magdalen to Fr Nivard, MSJA.

father was considering borrowing money by increasing his insurance money.' To add to the awkwardness of the occasion, Kevin's brother, Dermot, had himself entered Clonliffe the previous September. 'Despite everything we had a very gay Christmas holiday,' Kevin recalled. 'Although shy about being a "spoiled priest", I went to all the parties and dances.'

At this stage in his reminiscences, Kevin recalled an event that in reality may have occurred at an earlier date, since he mentions that he was nineteen years of age at the time. In any case, it scarcely reflects favourably on him. He had become friendly once more with a girl, kissing her and 'telling her it meant quite a lot' to him, but 'beyond that it did not go'.

> She had a patronising habit of treating me, and men generally, as children, and when I got to Dublin I wrote her some sort of letter assuring her of my affection and that this was not merely a holiday flirtation. I got back a very extraordinary letter, which either by design or by instinct, put me in the very humiliating position of saying I didn't mean it, or else to propose to her! It was very cleverly done, and she must have known by then how the family finances stood ... I had also decided that marriage was out for vocational reasons. As a result, I wrote some sort of angry letter, telling her not to be ridiculous, that it was very foolish to put a man in a corner, and she also should let him run things at his own pace etc., etc. That was the end of it. Frankly, I was amazed to be taken so seriously as that! I was prepared to be a good friend with her and in time to explore the possibilities of the situation. However, I felt very humiliated.

Before the end of Christmas 1923, it was decided that Kevin would return to Dublin to finish his science degree. He continued with his scholarship, and he was also able to draw for another two years on a County Council Scholarship he had won, which brought in £15 a year. He had also picked up between £15 and £20 annually in prizes, 'but unfortunately, instead of paying the Clonliffe bill, my mother had spent the money on family accounts'. Back in Dublin, Kevin stayed once more with his aunt at Rathmines.

Some months later, in April 1924, the Boylan family moved to Dublin. They stayed in a flat for some time before, in October 1924, obtaining a house in Longford Terrace, Monkstown, where they all lived once again under the same roof.

A LAY STUDENT AT UCD

Returning to university as a lay student, Kevin met regularly with his former classmate, Donal Flood, who lived quite near to his aunt's house in Rathmines. Flood later sketched an interesting pen-picture of his young friend at that time, although it is surprisingly silent on one subject. The country had only recently emerged from a civil war, there was widespread industrial unrest in Dublin, and the Free State government was endeavouring to establish order and stability in the young state. Yet none of this is reflected in Flood's account, or indeed in Kevin's own recollections.

Flood records that Kevin, on returning to UCD as a lay student, concentrated on physics, whereas he himself, a year ahead of Kevin, focused on chemistry. Kevin took part 'in all the activities of the university'. He was a member of the Literary and Historical Society, and 'he was, I think, secretary of the Scientific Society, if not secretary he was a very active member. He was in the Musical Society, and the Swimming Club ... He went to a lot of dances.' Flood also recalls that Kevin 'was also pally with what would have been regarded at the time as the top society in the college ... a crowd composed of the McGilligans, that is the younger fry of the Minister, you know, the O'Mearas, and several others who formed a sort of little group.'[26] Flood then clarifies, 'Kevin wasn't one of the group, but, unlike most other students, he kept contact with them. They rather looked down on the rest of us, I am afraid.'

The Musical Society was a natural outlet for Kevin. 'I wouldn't

---

26 The McGilligans referred to were the family of Patrick McGilligan, BL, TD, a very able minister of government. The O'Mearas were a wealthy business family from Limerick who played a prominent part in the struggle for political independence, and whose leading members had taken different sides in the Civil War.

describe him as being very musical', Flood recalled.

> He was something like myself ... We both had come
> from mothers who were extremely talented ... He was
> rather what Macauley would call meretricious in his
> performance, that is to say he had gloss; and that held,
> I think, in regard to everything he did. He had, I think,
> a highly developed sense of showmanship ... not in any
> derogatory sense, but he was adept at putting his best foot
> forward. I remember that after the Musical Society a few
> of us (would go) with Professor Cleary, who was an active
> member of the Society, over to his flat in Pembroke Rd
> and Kevin used to play the piano there. He would gloss
> over his faults very satisfactorily. I mention that merely as
> a point in his general character or personality. Another
> point that occurs to me ... he was individualistic, as I
> have said, and I would add that he was also highly
> unpredictable. For that reason, he did not tend to make
> close friends ... We both had the same sort of background
> on the musical side, so maybe I am like that myself.

Flood then added that Kevin 'had contacts with all the important people in our college life ... all the chaps that were on top'. He singled out a namesake of his, J. C. Flood, to whom was not related, for special mention. J. C. Flood was 'a very extraordinary character'. Kevin 'had a closer contact with him than with most other people ... Flood made no friends but made plenty of enemies. He seemed to attract Kevin Boylan, which is interesting in its way.' J. C. Flood will come up again in Boylan's story.

Continuing his reminiscences, Donal Flood remarked that, rather to his amazement, Kevin 'became quite a ladies' man ... There were several of those girls in the McGilligan group to whom he seemed quite attractive, and he told me so, as we were in fact quite confidential, but there was no question of love affairs or anything of the sort, of course, but it still was there and it did not seem to be in character with his subsequent development or his earlier promise'. That he might appear attractive to young women is indirectly supported by Flood's description of Kevin as 'a very fine-looking chap, a very handsome chap … He had a very attractive manner, a very pleasant address'. He adds that 'everybody knew him'.

One young woman, who had been a contemporary of Kevin's at the university, wrote to the monks of Roscrea after his death about her memories of him. 'I can still remember the respect in which we all held him. In some ways he was apart from all the others. I think now that he was probably much more mature than the rest of us although he was still very young. He was active as secretary of the Scientific Society and I can still see him, in dinner jacket, at the inaugural meeting!'[27] Kevin's sister, Kathleen, remarked that he held women in high esteem, and that 'he even knocked down a man before a crowd of others in UCD for speaking disrespectfully of one of the girls, even though the lady in question may not have been above reproach'. She added, 'He could be fiery and hot and was always what we called "jumpy"'.[28]

Asked by his interviewer if he would he describe Kevin as popular at the university, Flood replied, 'No, I would say he was not popular. He was well known but not popular … He was too individualistic … too unpredictable … in the sense that he'd be hail-fellow-well-met with you today, and tomorrow he'd be quite different, having met someone more important.' Flood elaborated further, 'I don't think he bothered about people or their feelings sufficiently … In a sense he would court favour with people but not in the way that men become popular, it was a little obvious. No, he was not popular, but everybody knew him.' He was, however, 'one of the leading people in the university', and 'he was very ambitious to get on'. Among other ambitions, 'he hoped to make the international swimming team'.

Towards the close of the interview, when asked if he considered Kevin to be brilliant at the university, Flood replied frankly, 'Brilliant in a meretricious way again … Yes, he was brilliant … but it was more the brilliance of imitation gold than that of real depth … I am

---

27 Eva White (née McDonald), 22 Richmond Avenue, Monkstown to Fr Nivard, 3 August 1964, MSJA.
28 Magdalen to Fr Nivard, MSJA.

giving what I believe is an honest opinion ... I certainly would not put him among the extremely brilliant ... There were more brilliant people in the university ... in the sense that they had more depth ... but that is only a personal opinion.'

After five years, Flood moved to the United State of America for his post-graduate studies. He met Kevin only seldom after that.

Despite his many interests and activities, Kevin did well in his studies. In 1925 he gained his M.Sc. degree for a thesis entitled *On the Large Ions of the Atmosphere*. Specialising in atmospheric electricity, he later produced a paper 'On Large Ions and Condensation Nuclei' which won him a travelling studentship in physics.[29] This was to result in a widening of his vision and an important expansion of his experience and knowledge. Nevertheless, it seems likely that the most formative factor in his university career was his participation in the Literary and Historical Society of UCD.

AT THE LITERARY AND HISTORICAL SOCIETY

It seems that Kevin attended meetings of the 'L & H' – as it was known – even while at Clonliffe. The auditor of the society for 1921–22, John Mowbray, wrote that Kevin 'was always listened to with that quiet respect that is accorded to a preacher by a person who thought he was getting a short Mass and suddenly discovered he had to listen to a sermon. He will go down in the history of the L & H as the only one of the members who ever took a vow of silence.'[30]

It was during the term of a later auditor, J. C. Flood (1923–24) – described by Mowbray as leaving 'an indelible mark on the Society' – that Kevin first flourished. 'There were many new faces in the Society,' Flood recalled, 'who were happily developing in speaking and in their power to get and hold the ear of the House: Hooper, Kevin Boylan, Roche, Max McKenna, who was to succeed me, The O'Rahilly, and Bill Sweetman, a truly gifted and versatile

---

29 Matt Hoehn (ed.), 'Eugene Boylan, OCSO, 1904–1964' in *Catholic Authors. Contemporary Biographical Sketches* (New Jersey: St Mary's Abbey, 1952), p. 36.

30 James Meenan (ed.), *Centenary History of the Literary & Historical Society, 1855–1955* (Dublin: A. & A. Farmer, 2005 ed.), p. 146.

mind ... I appointed a new official, a leader of the House. Kevin Boylan held the post. He liked the job and he drew fire that would otherwise have been directed higher up.'[31]

Kevin even took on the redoubtable J. C. Flood, 'whose caustic tongue was a legend in Dublin'.[32] P. F. Donovan, a committee member from 1925 to 1926, recalled that 'in October 1924 the personality of J. C. Flood still dominated the contemporary scene although his auditorial term was finished and that of his successor Max McKenna had successfully begun. His (Flood's) influence was to continue until broken by his friend and equal, Kevin Boylan. After a conflict of powerful personalities, in what in retrospect might be thought of as *une querelle des moines,* Flood temporarily abandoned his old love and founded a schismatic Legal & Economic Society ... it did not flourish. The great Flood never fully recovered his prestige and power in the Old Society.'[33] Suddenly, as it were, the young Boylan appears in a new light. Here was a good-looking man, an exciting and confident personality, colourful and flamboyant, prepared to take on the House.

The election for the next auditor took place in October 1925, and was won by Tony Malone by the slenderest of margins. He, unaccountably, resigned the following month, and in the resulting election Kevin Boylan was elected unanimously. With his good singing and speaking voice, Kevin had developed a powerful and commanding delivery, which helped him to win the Society's gold medals for oratory and impromptu debate.

In the tradition of his mother, her auditor son decided to do things in style. His inaugural address, in 1925, was influenced by his reading and his social interest at the time. He later explained, 'At the university, a growing interest in the social question and the problems of democratic government, especially that of power without responsibility, led me to Chesterton and Belloc; and it was G.K.C. who first gave me a relish for style, though I was

31 Meenan, *Centenary History*, pp. 157–8.
32 Meenan, *Centenary History*, p. xiv.
33 Meenan *Centenary History*, p.163.

far more concerned with his policy of distributism.'[34] The subject of the inaugural address was 'Democracy', and it was written in the hope of getting G. K. Chesterton himself to speak at the meeting. Unfortunately, it proved impossible to make the necessary arrangements for Chesterton to speak.

Undismayed, Kevin made his mark as auditor in another direction. As recalled by P. F. Donovan, he 'developed the modern series of inter-debates between the sister colleges of our university and Trinity and Queen's Belfast. In one of those debates the Irish language was saved or revived by northern eloquence and the votes of the Queen's students, the host on this occasion. From this beginning was developed the idea of international debates.'[35]

J. C. Flood remained friendly with Kevin, and he continued to attend the Literary and Historical Society for years after he had graduated.[36] His remarks about the Society were to find an echo in Eugene's own experience: 'The L & H was one of the formative influences of my youth as it has been for so many others'. Then he added, 'Incidentally, who would have foreseen that Skehan, Brian Dillon, Boylan and myself would end up as priests, the last three as monks? It was in the L & H that so many of us learnt our potential value and learnt, too, that there is a scale in human values that transcends the alignments of family, race, party and politics.'[37]

Flood joined the Benedictines in England, becoming Dom Peter Flood of Ealing Abbey. Describing a later encounter with Dom Eugene Boylan, he wrote, 'He is still very much L & H; does one ever lose it?'[38]

LEAVING UCD

In his final years at UCD, Kevin was appointed a student demonstrator. He was remembered as pleasant, easy-going and alive to the uncertainty and shyness of students who were only beginning

---

34 Hoehn, *Catholic Authors*, pp. 36–37.
35 Meenan, *Centenary History*, p. 163.
36 Meenan, *Centenary History*, p. xiv.
37 Meenan *Centenary History*, p. 161
38 Meenan, *Centenary History*, p. xiv.

in the university. As his sister Kathleen remarked of him in his dealings with students on a one-to-one basis, 'It was strange that one so greatly inclined to impatience could be such a good teacher'.[39] Kevin concluded his student career at University College Dublin with a travelling studentship in Physics, and subsequently applied for and obtained a Rockefeller Fellowship. These entitled him to study abroad for three years.

Kevin eagerly embraced the prospect of studying abroad, even though parting from home was difficult. His family were still in some financial difficulty: his father's pension was inadequate, and his mother made up what was needed by taking classes in piano and singing, especially in choral singing. With her ability and pleasantly commanding personality, she became a prominent figure in musical circles. 'Year after year,' it was reported, 'she was a familiar figure on the platforms or at the adjudicators' table at the leading Feiseanna.'[40] Kevin always spoke warmly and affectionately of her, and enjoyed telling stories about her and her unconventional ways, many of which surprised the neighbours. He also added that his father was 'the St Joseph of our house'.[41]

Kevin's studentship gave him a range of European universities from which to choose. He opted for Vienna because, as he admitted to a friend, 'he could not stand being patronised by the English', which he was sure would happen if he went to a British university.[42] The Irish Free State was but five years in existence at the time, and the memories of the struggle for freedom were still fresh. Vienna, with its cultural aura and high reputation in science, was particularly attractive. He felt he would be accepted as an equal there.

When Kevin said goodbye to the family, he approached his father last. Many years later, he recalled the scene with the utmost clarity. 'We were living at Monkstown at the time ... He was in the drawing room and I went in and said, "Well ... I'm off ... Goodbye Dad". Dad embraced me and shook hands and said "Goodbye Kevin,

39   Magdalen to Fr Nivard, MSJA.
40   Newspaper obituary, MSJA. No date or name of newspaper.
41   Eugene Boylan's typed manuscript account of his early years, MSJA.
42   Eugene Boylan's typed manuscript account of his early years, MSJA.

mind yourself and be nice to the prostitutes".' Kevin was struck by this unusual remark of his father, seemingly said in jest, and he saw a special significance in it. He commented in his later reflections, 'I tell you this to show you what a tremendous person my father was. Those were the words of a saint, you know!'[43]

As Kevin set out, the Boylan family were proud of his achievements, and excited at the prospect of his studying in Vienna, a city with such a wealth of musical and historical associations.

---

43 Fr Nivard Kinsella, typed document entitled 'Vienna', MSJA. Reflects the work and memories of Fr Nivard Kinsella.

CHAPTER 3

THE YEARS IN VIENNA, 1926–29

Vienna was in many ways a city of dreams to a musical family like the Boylans. It was the city of Gluck, Haydn, Mozart, Beethoven, Schubert, Brahms and Johann Strauss, and writers waxed lyrical about its beauty. Its population of two million was sufficiently large to yield 'all the diversity of a metropolis' but not so oversized as to be cut off from nature, like London or New York. 'The last houses of the city mirrored themselves in the mighty Danube or looked out over the wide plains, or dissolved themselves in gardens and fields, or climbed in gradual rises the last green wooded foothills of the Alps.'[44]

A CITY IN CRISIS

By the time Eugene arrived, Vienna was also a city in crisis. The glories of the Austro-Hungarian Empire had largely disappeared with its dismemberment at the end of the First World War. Austria had become a small state which was finding it difficult to survive economically, yet forbidden by the League of Nations from coalescing with its neighbour, Germany. In the years after the war, Austria, like Hungary and Bavaria, came to be dominated by radical Marxists. The socialist regime in Austria, faced with great problems of poverty, unemployment and a housing shortage, undertook a major building programme in Vienna. Solid, fortress-like flats, which were comfortable within, were constructed, the flagship of which was the striking Karl Marx-Hof in Heiligenstadt. The government was Marxist in philosophy, and anti-Christian and anti-bourgeois in outlook and practice. It did much to benefit the working-class population, but numerous Christian workers were cast out of their jobs. In its operation the government was also financially reckless, with industry being brought practically to a standstill. This led to a change of regime.

---

44 Stefan Zweig, *The World of Yesterday* (Lincoln: University of Nebraska Press, 1964), p. 13.

By 1925, the year before Kevin arrived in Vienna, a new government with a Christian Social majority had been formed, and financial stability was restored. Despite that, however, there was much unrest in the city during Kevin's years there. The opposition of the socialists resulted in strike after strike and the undermining of the economy. An unofficial socialist army, the Republikanischer Schutzbund, was active in challenging the government, and in July 1927 a general strike was declared in the administrative services, affecting the gas and electricity supplies. Riots ensued; efforts were made to storm the parliament buildings and, elsewhere in the city, the police were fired on and the law courts were set on fire. Against the odds, the police managed to hold out, and after three days the strike was broken; but it had been a touch-and-go affair. A key factor in the defeat of the strike was the anti-socialist gathering of volunteers known as the Heimwehr, an organisation which later became fascist in sympathy.

In the midst of the crisis, the chancellor, Dr Ignaz Seipel, a remarkable clergyman, remained calm and resolute.[45] Public confidence in him personally remained high, but the same could not be said about the political parties. With little confidence in them, the public looked to different extra-parliamentary bodies. The Heimwehr, in particular, grew in popularity. In April 1929, Kevin's last year in Vienna, Dr Seipel resigned. The following August, there was a head-on clash between the Schutzbund and the Heimwehr, and towards the end of 1929 the government resigned. Parliamentarianism had been discredited, and a period of turmoil followed. Eventually, in 1932, Engelbert Dollfuss became president, only to be assassinated by a Nazi organisation in 1934. By then, Kevin had been back in Ireland for some five years.

ARRIVAL IN VIENNA

There is no direct reference to any of the foregoing in Kevin's extant correspondence, although he must have been aware of much that was going on politically during the years 1926–29. Many years

45   J. D. Gregory, *Dollfuss and his Times* (London: Hutchinson, 1935), pp. 130–31.

later, however, while recalling his time in Vienna, Kevin expressed a strong conviction about those days, suggesting that he was indeed aware of the wider political scene at the time.

> In Vienna I tried my hand at journalism by acting as a correspondent for an Irish Catholic weekly, for which I afterwards did some music critiques. I soon became aware of the appalling misrepresentation which continental news and especially Catholic news suffered at the pens of English-speaking journalists. They made no secret that they had to write nothing but what their editors, proprietors, or advertisers wanted to publish, and most of them suffered from an absolute inability to see events and institutions other than in terms of their own provincialism. They were all prisoners of their time and of the temper of their readers. The fight made by Monsignor Seipel and Dollfuss to save Austria from Communism and Nazism got no sympathy or help from them.[46]

Apart from this comment, all the indications are that Kevin's life was largely taken up by his studies and by his enjoyment of the music and culture of this great European city. He looked back on his time in Vienna, as he had on his youth in Monkstown, as 'halcyon years' in his life.

A priority for an effective life in Austria was to learn the German language. 'To read for the studentship,' he observed, 'I had needed French, and life in Vienna made German necessary, so I had to teach myself these two languages. But even when I had acquired a certain facility in reading German I never turned to literature for reading.' His attitude to learning the language and his confidence in his capacity to succeed were illustrated by the remarks of Fr Nivard Kinsella OCSO, who would later come to know Kevin in Roscrea.

> Just before he left Ireland someone asked him about his knowledge of German. 'None,' he replied, 'but I am taking this with me to read on the way', pulling a copy of Hugo's *Self-Tuition* out of his pocket. He claimed afterwards that

---

46 Hoehn, *Catholic Authors*, p. 37.

by the time he began work at the university he had learned enough of the language from the little book to enable him to work without too much difficulty, and then living in the city and mixing with people he rapidly acquired fluency. This fluency in German remained with him to the end of his life, and it was remarked on by all who knew him in Vienna that no topic and no level of conversation was beyond him. Thirty years later he could follow the German radio with ease and pleasure. His brother, Gerald, remembered him, during the summer which Kevin spent at home on leave from Vienna, explaining the difference of usage between the urban German of Vienna and the local dialects of the countryside, with a surprising amount of information about the genesis of such linguistic differences. This was typical of his approach to anything, and he would never have been content with a mere speaking knowledge of the language.[47]

On arriving in the city, Kevin was fortunate to find lodgings in a small *pensione* not far from the university. There was a little church nearby where he attended Mass each day. Years later as abbot, when returning from a general chapter in Rome, he visited Vienna and celebrated Mass in this church. 'Here, he said, he had got his vocation'.[48] At the university, he discovered that he was the only Irishman studying there; nevertheless he soon settled in, finding his work absorbing. He studied under Professor Egon von Schweidler and subsequently in the Radium Institute, Vienna, under Professor Stefan Meyer.[49] About his work, Kevin recalled that he was 'in close touch with the research on cosmic rays and atomic disintegration, and I studied various techniques on equipment for future research.'[50] While applying himself to his studies, he does not appear to have brought his work back to the *pensione* with him, leaving him time to savour student life and the musical culture of Vienna.

47 Fr Nivard, typed manuscript entitled 'Vienna', MSJA.
48 Fr Nivard, typed manuscript entitled 'Vienna', MSJA. .
49 Information obtained from the O'Connell School Magazine, 1929, MSJA.
50 Nash, 'Dom Eugene Boylan' in *Ten More Priests*, p. 18.

ENJOYING STUDENT LIFE

After a number of months, some other Irish students arrived who were enrolled in the faculty of medicine or psychology. The usual procedure for English-speaking medical students at the time was for them to join the American Medical Association. Shortly after their arrival two of these new arrivals recalled having letters delivered to them at the Association, saying that there was an Irishman in the city who would be glad to meet them.[51] By then Kevin was friendly with a number of families in the city and was happy to show the newcomers its many points of interest.

One such student, whom he met in his final year in the city, had very happy memories of their time together. His account provides a brief cameo of Boylan's lifestyle at the time. On 19 August 1964, Dr Michael P. Fay wrote from Edenderry, Co. Offaly, to Fr Nivard in Roscrea:

> I was in Vienna from January to May 1929, doing a post graduate medical course. Shortly after my arrival there I received a note signed Kevin Boylan asking me to meet with him. I became very friendly with Kevin Boylan as I then knew him. He was a very gay and charming companion, and we went many places together. These included concerts, opera, theatres, and even beer gardens. On one occasion we went to Budapest for a long weekend with some friends of his who came to Vienna for a holiday. I have never forgotten my time in Vienna. It was a very happy time in my life and due in great part to my meeting with him. I visited his mother in Dún Laoghaire on occasions, after I had returned.[52]

'Vienna gave me a feast of music', Boylan later said.[53] Like most students he tended to be short of cash, so he and a friend would stand in the cheapest part of the Opera House, following the music in a score which they shared between them, since they could only

51   Fr Nivard, typed manuscript entitled 'Vienna', MSJA.
52   Dr. M. P. Fay to Fr Nivard Kinsella, 19 August 1964, MSJA.
53   Hoehn, *Catholic Authors*, p. 37.

afford one copy.[54] Poverty among students was a feature of life in Vienna. One English author, writing in the early 1930s, observed that 'in many Austrian universities students are still compelled to go from house to house begging, and as a rule the charity of those who have something to give … is unfailing.'[55] Kevin benefitted from the same tolerant and generous spirit towards students. For a long period, he dined every evening at the Augustinerkeller in company with another Irish student. They got to know the head waiter, and the same table was kept for them each evening. They would meet at eight o'clock at the corner of one of the principal squares and walk to their destination. Boylan liked to drink wine, and during his time in Vienna he became knowledgeable about wines. It was his only drink, apart from a liqueur after dinner on special occasions. 'You can know how much wine you can drink,' he remarked, 'but spirits can knock you over without your realising it'. [56]

It is a measure of the poverty in the city at that time, and of the tolerance of the restauranteurs, that beggars frequented restaurants moving from table to table. They were usually well-mannered. 'The first impressions of Vienna', Cicely Hamilton wrote in the 1920s, 'is poverty and hardship, far from the romantic image of imperial days. Life continued hard and uncertain for a great many people. There was little spare money.' People could not afford to buy motor cars. 'As a result, the roads were quiet,' and it was 'easy to cross the road almost anywhere'. Yet, despite the hardships of life, the cult of the old Vienna was popular. Postcards and prints of a bygone age could be found, with people sometimes dressed up in the garb of a previous century. Festivals of the old Vienna were re-enacted. 'In no other city with which I am acquainted', Ms Hamilton observed, 'are the life and manners of a bygone age so frequently brought to your notice.'[57] Nowhere was this more evident than in the splendour of the opera, which the city maintained against all adversity.

54   Kinsella, *Dom Eugene Boylan*, p.3.
55   J. D. Gregory, *Dollfuss and his Times*, p.90.
56   Fr Nivard, typed manuscript entitled 'Vienna', MSJA.
57   Cicely Hamilton, *Modern Austria as Seen by an Englishwoman* (London: J.M. Dent & Sons, 1935), pp. 27, 35–37.

The celebrated Viennese author, Stefan Zweig, proudly proclaimed, 'Every one of us has, from his youthful years, brought a strict and inexorable standard of musical performance into his life ... Gustav Mahler's discipline down to the minutest detail in the Opera House, and the energetic exactitude of the Philharmonic followed and set standards ... Whoever lived in Vienna caught a feeling of rhythm from the air ...'[58] Kevin Boylan, with his love of music, was heir to all this.

A MAN OF SEEMING CONTRADICTIONS

Not many of Kevin's letters from *Wien*, as he regularly termed the city, have survived. Some that were written during a Whit weekend, probably in 1927, have come down to us, however, and these, while informal, prove to be informative. Addressing his mother as *Meine Liebe Mutter*, he wrote:

> I am writing this in my pyjamas, and only inborn respect for convention keeps me from writing it in my pelt. The weather here has been very changeable and yesterday it became frightfully hot – 95F in the shade! Today, it passed 100 degrees. The worst part of it is that the breeze is hotter than the still air. Work is out of the question, so that I'm clearing out tomorrow morning if I can get up to catch the 7.30 boat, which leaves at about an hour's drive from here up the river to a place called Melk ... I believe it may be important to get a room for the night there but I'm taking my chances. I'll probably have to sleep in a peasant's hut – but no matter. Yesterday evening was so hot that I cleared out to the Old Danube, stripped down to a pair of 3 cornered things, got on an old boat, went out to the middle of the river, where I remained for 3 or 4 hours – dropping into the water every ten minutes to keep cool.

The following day, Whit Saturday, he added to the letter from Hotel Melkerhof:

58 S. Zweig, *The World of Yesterday*, pp. 19–20.

Having got up in time to catch the aforesaid boat, I, of
course, forgot to post your letter. I had a lovely trip up the
river. Between this and *Wien* is said to be the nicest part
of the Danube. But, unfortunately, the weather seems to
be changing. With a few exceptions, I was the only man
on the boat wearing long trousers. All the old Austrians
don shorts, bare knees, and travel in their shirt sleeves,
consuming large quantities of beer and sausages on the way
up ... Everybody told me that it was out of the question
to get into a hotel but I rushed to be first off of the boat
crowd. I walked in here and got the last room in the best
hotel in Melk.

Kevin continued:

There is a wonderful old monastery here. I see they have
High Mass at 8 o'c with special music tomorrow. I believe
the monastery is well worth exploring. The favourite game
here in this weather is to get any old boat, bring it up river
with the ship, and drift down again. I was invited by the
Swimming Club crowd to come up to Linz (about 150
miles from *Wien*) and drift down, but I cried off – I mean
3 days forced intimacy with strangers talking another
language!

Things are going well here, but nothing exciting. I
played a trial water-polo game with a local club and I'll get
my fill of polo now. The swimming is coming on remarkably.
A little faster, I think, but much easier. My trainer's great
motto is – 'no force or strength to be used' (he calls it *kraft*).
My tonsillitis has completely disappeared.

How is everybody at home? ... I was dreaming about
Tim last night. Glamorgan don't seem to be doing all that
wonderfully, though I see Ryan did some good bowling
against Northampton. No vote has come for the election
[to the university panel in the Irish Senate] although I got
a letter this morning asking me to vote no.1 for McNeill [a
government minister and former professor of Irish History

in University College Dublin]. I'm very interested to know how the election turns out. If I get hold of a voting paper I'll vote 'agin' the government. I'm sorry this letter is in pencil, but I've no ink and I wanted to drop you a line before I went away (trip of 2 or 3 days). Best of luck with the Derby (perhaps it's all over by now). If you cannot read this, dip it in water.[59]

Kevin stood out as one of the few Irishmen in the university, but also because he was active in a number of student bodies, loved to argue, made no enemies and was generally liked. He attended student dances and, as usual, was popular with women students, but was not involved exclusively with any one of them. As in UCD, the women he mingled with were from prominent families. One such was a certain Fräulein Adler, daughter of a celebrated father. Alfred Adler (1870–1937) was a medical doctor, psychotherapist, and founder of Adlerian psychology – sometime termed Individual Psychology – who lectured extensively in Europe and the United States.[60] For a time, Fräulein Adler was Kevin's usual companion at dances, but he also took delight in the intellectual atmosphere of the Adler home. It is recorded that on one occasion, as Kevin waited for Fräulein Adler to come downstairs and accompany him to a dance, he got into conversation with her father. Dr Adler enquired if he were the Irish physicist about whom he had heard, and on receiving an affirmative answer asked him how he could be both a physicist and a believer in God. It was a question for which Kevin was well prepared, for he had faced it himself long since. A long discussion ensued, which was eventually interrupted by the Fräulein asking Kevin somewhat coldly if he had come to discuss religion with her father or to take her to a dance.[61]

Religion continued to play a major part in Kevin's life. He attended Mass at his local church on weekdays. Sometimes, after

59 Eugene to his mother, MSJA. 'Feast of Coemge', no date. The second part of the letter is dated Whit Saturday.
60 In the 1930s, when Adler's Austrian clinics were closed by the Nazis because of his Jewish heritage, he moved to the US. He died in 1937 during a lecture visit to Scotland.
61 Fr Nivard, typed manuscript entitled 'Vienna', MSJA. .

a late night, he would go to the eleven o'clock Mass, even though it meant fasting in order to receive communion.[62] On his own admission, he attended High Mass in the churches of Vienna on Sundays in order to enjoy the choirs and string orchestras. During those years, it is not clear if he thought of entering a religious congregation or once again considered becoming a priest. It was a standing joke with one of his companions that, whenever the conversation turned to the future and their prospects, Boylan would say that he intended entering the Jesuits as soon as he got back to Ireland. Just how serious he was about this it is difficult to say.

Everyone remembered him as a religious man – more so than the average student – but at the same time, as ever, there seemed to be contradictory aspects to his character. In the words of one of his contemporaries, 'he was a peculiar mixture. He would sit up all night, very often until three in the morning, talking about religion, politics, philosophy, everything. He would argue and disagree about everything, and whatever you said would be dissected and analysed. But he had a profound faith, and whenever we were out walking together he would rarely pass a church without popping in for a minute. It was very striking in that most of the physicists one met tended to be agnostics. Boylan found no difficulty at all in reconciling a very profound and living faith with all the rationalism of the scientist.'[63]

An indication of his reflective, spiritual side appears in the following extracts from two of his letters, written from Vienna to his younger sister, Kathleen. She had entered the Cistercian convent at Glencairn, Co. Waterford, and had written to him from there. In his reply, dated 19 June 1928, Kevin remarked, 'You seem to be wonderfully happy. Don't be alarmed if you get a bit depressed at times,' for 'religion loses all its consolation. Make an act of faith, hope and charity, and soon all will be in order.' He suggested the following aspiration 'as the best method of conquering and getting rid of trials – "My God, I thank Thee that things are not going

62 Magdalen to Fr Nivard, MSJA.
63 Fr Nivard, typed manuscript entitled 'Vienna', MSJA.

my way". That seems to be all God wants, because once one says that from the heart, immediately gloom begins to lighten and the trials run away.' Just over seven months later, when Kathleen – now known as Magdalen – was experiencing difficulty and some form of suffering in her religious life, he empathised with her, adding, 'Of course one has to suffer – who can love and not suffer? ... It seems to be that suffering is the expression of love, and that that is a very helpful view of the Incarnation.'

Kevin's religion was never ostentatious, however, and no one would have thought of him as pious. He was full of vitality and, as already indicated, was good company, an engaging conversationalist, a lover of music, a frequenter of beer cellars and of the *heurigen*,[64] fond of social life generally, and a favourite with women students. He dated some, but generally went out in a party and seemed to have no thought of settling down. His fellow students recalled an occasion when two women fought a duel over him; Kevin, it is said, fled from both of them.

Another incident left a more lasting impression on him. Returning from a party one night, he saw a young woman to her lodgings. Having kissed goodnight, Kevin turned to go home only to be rebuked by the woman for accepting her kiss; she claimed it was tantamount on his part to asking for further intimacy, and on hers to granting it. The erstwhile carefree student left her a chastened and confused young man. The memory remained with him and influenced his thinking. He is said to have recalled this incident when writing about moral theology, and particularly in his reference to the probable differences that would exist between an Eskimo theologian and one from Central Europe on the morality of kissing.[65]

A further occasion of embarrassment occurred one evening as he was walking in the city with a friend. They stopped to admire a display of shoes in a shop window. The shoes were made of snake skin, and as an advertising gambit there was a live snake in a glass

---

64   *Heurigen* are inns that serve the new wine at harvest time.
65   Fr Nivard, typed manuscript entitled 'Vienna', MSJA.

tank in the window. After looking at the display for a few moments, Boylan suddenly noticed the snake and fled in horror, not stopping until he had put two blocks between himself and the shop. He afterwards admitted to having an intense aversion to snakes that was almost pathological, saying that he was unable to control his reaction on this occasion. It may well be that such vulnerability helped him develop that sympathy for weaknesses and peculiarities in others that was a marked feature in his later life.

Among Kevin's other unusual experiences in Vienna was his involvement in a duel. He and another Irishman were entertaining Kevin's landlady to dinner at a resort just outside the city. In the course of the meal they got into conversation with a couple at the next table, who at the end of the evening offered them a lift home. It is not clear if the landlady joined them, but the two Irishmen gladly accepted. On finding that the car was a chauffeur-driven Rolls Royce, Kevin's companion made some seemingly innocuous remark. The owner of the car took offence, however, and punched him on the nose. Kevin had to separate the two men, and the couple eventually drove off, leaving the two students to make their own way home.

Presuming the incident closed, Kevin was surprised the next morning when his friend arrived at his lodging with a note from their companion of the previous night challenging him to a duel. The weapons were to be cavalry sabres, and the challenger was awaiting a reply. Kevin was taken aback and his friend was distressed. On consideration, however, Kevin suggested that the only thing to do was to accept the challenge. Despite his sister's claim that 'he was always free from human respect',[66] Kevin's advice on this occasion arose from how others would perceive them. He argued that, as the only two Irishmen in the university at the time, they might as well leave the city straightaway if they refused the duel, as they would never again be able to appear in public. Appalled at this advice, his friend began to imagine himself being cut to pieces. Kevin announced, however, that he would act as second, and that he would get an acquaintance at the Cavalry School to teach his friend how

66 Magdalen to Fr Nivard, MSJA.

to use the sabre. The challenge was accepted and a date fixed for the following week. Kevin then brought his companion to the Cavalry School in preparation.

The duellists met as arranged. The Irishman, deciding that attack was the best method of defence, came out fiercely swinging his sabre, and it was he who drew first blood. With that, the protagonists gravely shook hands and departed the scene. Honour was satisfied, and the two Irish students reappeared at the university having proudly upheld the honour of the student body.[67]

OUTWARD APPEARANCE AND THE INNER SELF

Photos of Kevin's time in Vienna show him, during the spring and summer, boating on the Danube and looking down over the city of Buda. In the winter, we see him tobogganing and skating, but not skiing, since skis were beyond his means. Some mountain climbing also featured in his pastimes.

His love of music, and the emphasis in Vienna on acquiring high standards, led him to seek lessons in the piano. His family benefitted from these when he came home. 'He had a passion for playing the piano,' Kathleen reported. 'Fortunately, he was quite good ... especially after coming home from Vienna where he had a few lesson and heard the best musicians. We used to think that he solved all his problems on the piano (which was upstairs) – Chopin was a favourite and when we heard the triumphant tone of the "Polonaise" we felt that all was well in his world.'[68]

This then was Kevin Boylan in Vienna: light-hearted, but serious-minded at the same time; studying hard and enjoying it, but rarely talking about his studies outside class; a good mixer, ready to stay up late into the night debating all sorts of topics; fond of dancing and parties, attractive to women and a lover of music. He frequented not only the Opera House but the leading churches for High Mass on Sundays, when he could hear orchestras performing some of the works of the great composers and, occasionally, an

---

67 Fr Nivard, typed manuscript entitled 'Vienna', MSJA.
68 Magdalen to Fr Nivard, MSJA.

opera singer in the *Credo* or the *Agnus Dei*. Beneath the outward appearance, however, there was a man of strong, informed faith and religious outlook. Then, as later, none of his contemporaries knew what was going on within Kevin. He remained, as his sister Molly acutely remarked, 'somewhat withdrawn from others. Although he mixed around in the social world, one felt there was a mask over his real self'.[69]

---

69   Magdalen to Fr Nivard, MSJA.

PART II: 1929–60

CHAPTER 4

THE TRANSITION FROM UCD TO
ROSCREA ABBEY, 1929–33

In 1929 Kevin Boylan came back to Dublin, where he accepted a position as assistant lecturer in physics at University College Dublin. There he taught and did research for the next two years, publishing a further paper 'Atmospheric Ionization and Condensation Nuclei'.[70] A former graduate student, Vincent Moloney, who was not from the science faculty, remembered him clearly.

> I knew him well when he returned from Vienna … and often swam with him, principally at Dún Laoghaire. He was a powerful swimmer. He was then admired and greatly envied by all of us recent graduates. He had got an appointment straightaway at UCD and it appeared that he was exploring in a field in science which offered the greatest academic excitement, viz. the breaking of the atom.
>
> He was the gayest and most debonair of any of us. Just imagine when I next met him: I went to Mount St Joseph to teach in October 1931, and one day I met him shovelling – or at least trying to – at a muddy farm gap as one goes down towards the river from the monastery. He could not speak to me – he only laughed at his change of occupation.[71]

Moloney added that he later heard that Boylan 'explained his going to Mount St Joseph by saying that he fell in love with God. Such men are rare indeed.'[72]

In the years after his return to Dublin Kevin, behind the

---

70 Hoehn, *Catholic Authors,* p. 37.
71 Vincent Moloney to Fr Nivard, MSJA. No date, but 1964.
72 Moloney to Fr Nivard, MSJA.

debonair manner, took life seriously. From the rather disjointed notes of a talk he gave to the senior boys at O'Connell School,[73] it seems clear that he was concerned about the world-wide struggle between the materialism of contemporary life and the claims of the Catholic Church as the representative of Jesus Christ and his values. In this context, he spoke both of the dangers to the new Irish State and the leadership for good that it could give. He also expressed concern at the expanding urbanisation of Ireland and the impact this was having on rural communities. He stressed that technology appropriate to the real needs of Ireland needed to be developed or imported, so that Ireland and its people might prosper while preserving their spiritual heritage. He also strongly supported lay involvement in the development of the life of the Church.

About this time, Kevin was struggling with the thought of God's will for him in life. 'It's all right for you,' he told his married brother, Gerald, 'you know what God's will is in your case. But what does he want me to do?'[74] Kevin subsequently observed that during this time 'I was growing more and more conscious of the need of a firm foundation in scholastic philosophy and a training in the spiritual life. Neither was easy to find. I was also beginning to see the need for new methods and new organisations on the Catholic front ... The next two years brought a change in outlook. In various ways I discovered that persons were more important than things, and that the personal love of Our Lord matters more than any service however great. The question of a vocation, which was always in my mind, again came to the foreground.'[75]

He thought about making a short retreat at Mount St Joseph Abbey, Roscrea. It seems that he discussed this with his mother who, in turn, mentioned it to her friend, Dom Justin McCarthy, the abbot of Roscrea. She was not quite enthusiastic about the idea, it seems, but the abbot responded bluntly: 'Never mind what you think. Send

---

73 'Our Task' by R. K. Boylan, M.Sc., printed in the O'Connell School's magazine, pp. 33–36, MSJA. In MSJA the typed script is intermingled with later observations by Eugene expressing his views on Church and state and the Irish economy.
74 Nash, 'Dom Eugene Boylan' in *Ten More Priests*, p.22.
75 Hoehn, *Catholic Authors*, p. 37.

him on to us and we will give him every assistance to come to a decision on his future'. During Holy Week 1931, aged twenty-seven years, Kevin presented himself at the monastery's guesthouse. He was greeted by the Abbot, who appointed a priest to assist him in coming to a decision. At the end of the retreat Kevin had not made up his mind, but he expressed satisfaction with his days of quiet and prayer in the monastery, and asked if he might return at Whit for the same purpose.[76]

With his mother at Roscrea.

76 Dom Camillus Claffey, 'Dom Eugene Boylan,1904–1964' in 'Profiles in Sanctity', unpublished typed document, pp. 26, 28, MSJA.

In the fifty days between the two retreats, Kevin thought and prayed about God's will for him. He thought of entering one of the active religious orders, such as the Jesuits or the Dominicans, which seemed suited to his temperament and academic interests, but then he met with a Franciscan, a Fr Augustine, to whom he expressed his problem and who firmly advised him to join the Cistercian Order.[77] Kevin undertook his second retreat in Roscrea at Pentecost, during which he thought about his brother Dermot's choice of the Carthusians, and also about the Congregation of St Paul, in the USA, founded for the diffusion of good literature. During these retreats, his director was careful to avoid swaying him towards any particular order, and he was quite astonished when Kevin told him at the end of the retreat that he intended to join the monastery at Mount St Joseph.[78] Kevin obtained an appointment with the abbot and explained to him that he wished to join the monastery, giving an account of his background and his reasons for applying.

He received a firm refusal.[79] This was scarcely surprising. Kevin's vivacious temperament and style of life seemed at odds with life in a Cistercian monastery. If one visits one of their monasteries for a month or even a week, it becomes apparent that Cistercian routine is the unchanging. The monks are regularly occupied in choir according to a scheduled time-table, or else involved in manual labour or some particular work about the house. If one comes back a year later, it is clear that the same regime prevails. The food, meanwhile, is basic and silence prevails. The tranquillity of mind needed to live contentedly according to such a programme, day after day, is not given to everyone. In the light of Kevin's temperament and background, the abbot and his advisers had reason to doubt his suitability.

Kevin pleaded very hard that they not turn him away without

77 Nash, 'Dom Eugene Boylan' in *Ten More Priests*, p. 22. Claffey, 'Profiles in Sanctity', MSJA. Fr Nivard Kinsella in his booklet says that Kevin's Jesuit spiritual father encouraged him to go back to Roscrea to test out his vocation, p. 5.
78 Claffey, 'Profiles in Sanctity', p. 28, MSJA.
79 Nash, 'Dom Eugene Boylan' in *Ten More Priests*.

giving him a chance,[80] and when he was accepted as a postulant, he resigned as lecturer at UCD. At that time, he was advised to 'ask that this position be kept for him for two years' but, as he later informed his novice master, 'No … I burnt my boats'.[81] In July, shortly before joining the monastery, Kevin had entered for swimming and diving competitions in Blackrock. 'I suppose', he said to the Master of Novices, 'I must now abandon these'. 'On the contrary,' was the reply, 'go ahead and bring the medals with you.' He did.[82]

A rather amusing account of Kevin's final day before becoming a postulant was sent to Fr Nivard by a Br Stanislaus Burns OFM, on 16 August 1964.[83] He explained that he had been spending a few days at Mount St Joseph Abbey some thirty-three years earlier when he happened to meet Kevin.

> One evening as I strolled by the river on the Abbey grounds I chanced to meet a young man who introduced himself … We chatted for some time and later had a swim in the river and afterwards rested on the bank. It was then he told me that he was entering the Abbey as a postulant that night, and was anxious to dispose of all the cigarettes he had in his possession. We chain-smoked until all were finished.

Br Burns continued his story:

> I remember asking him his reasons for entering so strict an order and his reply was that he had witnessed so much laxity and irreligion among the students and professors while studying on the Continent, that he was determined to devote his time and talents in future to the service of God in the cloister … What impressed me most about him at that period was his spirit of sacrifice and his determination to surrender himself completely to the love of Jesus and all that it demanded of him.

80 Nash, 'Dom Eugene Boylan' in *Ten More Priests*, p. 23.
81 Claffey, 'Profiles in Sanctity', p. 28, MSJA.
82 Claffey, 'Dom Eugene Boylan' in 'Profiles in Sanctity', MSJA.
83 R. S. Burns to Fr Nivard, MSJA. Dated 28/8/64, from Franciscan monastery, Farragher, Co. Roscommon.

Given the frailty of human memory, especially at a distance of more than thirty years, and given Kevin's later popularity as a spiritual writer and lecturer, it is not unlikely that some of Br Burns's recollections were coloured by the passing of time. Nevertheless, the account of the meeting by the river bank and the final consumption of cigarettes sounds authentic as Kevin's goodbye to a way of life. The date was 8 September 1931. From the monastery records, the planned entry date had been changed from 15 August to 8 September, the feast of Our Lady's Nativity.

Significantly, Burns mentioned that Kevin 'spoke very enthusiastically about a little book by Fr Jaegar (*sic*) SJ, entitled *One with Jesus*, and recommended it strongly to me. Needless to say, I read it and found it most helpful in the path I had chosen to follow'. Later in life, as Eugene Boylan, he would single out that book on several occasions. Indeed, he would state, 'For our own part, the spiritual life had little meaning for us until we read *One With Jesus* by Fr De Jaegher SJ, to whom we are eternally indebted.'[84]

LIFE AS A NOVICE

After a month's postulancy, the abbot clothed Kevin with the Cistercian habit and gave him the name Eugene. His patron was Blessed Pope Eugene III (c.1080–1153), a former abbot, who had been formed at Clairvaux by St Bernard. Eugene Boylan then began his two years of noviceship. He had read widely before entering the monastery. On being given Adolphe Tanqueray's recently issued book, *The Spiritual Life*, he replied that he had finished it some time ago. When asked if he had ever read Alphonsus Rodriguez's *The Practice of Perfection and Christian Virtues* – a book by an old-fashioned author then standard in religious congregations – he replied, 'Yes, but never again'. In the words of Dom Camillus Claffey, Eugene was 'a prodigious reader ... In a short space he could read a book of five hundred pages. He seemed to absorb the text rather than read it.'[85]

84 Nash., *Catholic Authors*, p. 24; quoted from *This Tremendous Lover.*
85 Claffey, 'Profiles in Sanctity', p. 29.

As a novice at Roscrea.

As a novice, Eugene shared the fully arranged life of the community. In the course of an article in *Doctrine and Life*,[86] shortly before the Second Vatican Council (1962–65), he described that 'arranged life' as it existed at that time. The novice's day, he explained,

> starts a little after two o'clock in the morning, when he joins the community in the church for the choral recitation of Matins and Lauds and for half-an-hour's mental prayer. When, after that, the priests say Mass, he assists at Mass and receives Holy Communion. Returning to the school-like novitiate room, he can read until the monastic breakfast is served at about half-past five. Office of Prime is sung after six, and he joins the community in chapter to listen to the teaching of the superior of the monastery. The community High Mass, which is preceded by the office of Tierce, follows after a short interval; and then the community take themselves to their various employments. For the novice this generally means outdoor work in the fields or the garden – not strenuous or too exacting. The office of Sext is sung before dinner at eleven-thirty. More time for reading or study follows until the office of None, and there is another period of work from two until half-past three. Vespers are sung about four-fifteen, and a quarter of an hour's mental prayer follows. After that comes the light evening meal, then more time for study, then public reading for the whole community, followed by the office of Compline, and so to bed in a common dormitory at seven o'clock. Here he sleeps fully clothed, on a simple straw mattress, in the comparative privacy that a cubicle provides. For the rest of the day he lives in the constant presence of his brethren.[87]

It should be added that in those days the liturgy was in Latin, and that in addition to the long Divine Office the Office of Our Lady was recited, and on some days the Office of the Dead. There was a

---

86 E. Boylan, 'Path To Holiness: V. The Cistercians' in *Doctrine and Life*, June 1961, pp. 285ff.
87 E. Boylan, *Doctrine and Life*, pp. 285–6.

rule of silence which reigned even on Christmas Day. Most monks never spoke except to the abbot, the prior or the novice master – or if necessary when working with someone else, for example on book-binding. There was in existence, however, a very effective system of signs, which enabled everybody to get by; this meant that those who were proficient could communicate almost anything. The sign system contributed very effectively to the silence of the house, but not necessarily to the silence of the individual. The monks never had any special time for recreation, though they could manage to have fun through signs.

Eugene was one of the choir monks. In those years, there were also in the monastery the lay brothers, who had a different way of life. They wore a brown habit, distinct from the white of the choir monks covered by a black scapular, and they did not participate in the Divine Office. They had their own much simpler office of prayers and did not have a vote in community matters. They were mainly involved in manual work, for example on the farm or in the mills. After the Second Vatican Council the category of lay brother disappeared.[88]

Turning to asceticism and prayer, Eugene, in his article in *Doctrine and Life*, explained that the novice has 'three meals a day, if they can be called meals ... for not only is meat excluded, but also fish, while eggs are only allowed in cases of necessity. Not only are rules of silence characteristic of the Cistercian life, there is also a law of enclosure, which is quite strict. A serious reason is needed to justify permission to leave the monastery even for a few days.'

The novice, of course, received frequent instruction on 'the regulations of the order, on the spiritual life in general, and in particular on the teaching and spirit of St Benedict ... He has much time to read, and after two years as a novice he makes temporary vows of obedience, stability and improvement of manners for a period of three years. At the end of this three-year period, he and the community have to decide whether he will take solemn vows for life. This solemn profession, as it is called, is the crucial point of the monks' life.'

88   Fr Laurence Walsh, OCSO to Eugene, 27 August 2017.

Something likely to surprise the new novice was the little provision made for private prayer. 'The Divine Office takes four or five hours to sing, but apart from that, the novice is not encouraged to spend much time in the church.' Again, the earnest novice, who might be seeking greater discomforts and a more ascetical life, might be surprised to find 'that any tendency to add to the penitential practices of the life is severely frowned upon'. The great penance or asceticism for the monk is his obedience – to the rule, to God as represented in the superior, and in active acceptance of the monotony of routine. For St Benedict, obedience – the surrender of one's will to another for the sake of Christ – is, indeed, the primary asceticism. Benedict asks the beginner 'whether he truly seeks God, is he zealous for the Divine Office, does he wish for obedience and humility with all their difficulties?' The first of these is the important question, the older Eugene points out, for a monk must seek God above all; everything else is tributary to that. It takes the young monk a long time to realise 'that religious life is organised to give God not so much the monk's services as the monk's own self'. The second thing he must come to recognise is that in religious life, and especially in monastic life, 'what the religious does for God is not nearly so important as what God does for the religious'.

Continuing in that self-revelatory vein, Eugene stated that the monk's first conversion 'is to realise that the one thing required of him is personal love of God', and that all he does is empty 'except in so far as it comes from love'. Early in his monastic life the monk 'begins to discover the person of Jesus Christ, to know something of his intense love for each of us', and to give Jesus the love of his own heart. 'He begins to see the spiritual life as a partnership with Jesus, and if he is willing to make the sacrifices that such a partnership involves, he will soon find that Our Lord is generous in manifesting his love and interest in return.' Eugene then added that 'these graces do much to detach the monk from many things he previously held dear; and lead him to generosity in his monastic life. Obedience begins to appear in a new light, for he realises that in doing God's will, he will always have Jesus for his companion'.

During his two years as a novice, Eugene brought to his new studies the same intensity and seriousness that he had brought to his scientific studies. He explored 'every phase of what one calls the spiritual or higher way of life'.[89] Very particularly, he studied the founders of the Cistercian order and developed some of the insights that were a feature of his later distinctive spirituality.[90]

The excitement of research and reading, however, could not overcome the many dark hours he spent when the austere silence, the loneliness, the stark surroundings and the routine that blunted the spirit all weighed him down. At such times the appeal of home, the companionship of women and men, and the excitement and music of Vienna shone with a special allure. Especially on Sunday mornings, when rows of cars brought people to the monastery's church for Mass, the novice was tempted to ask himself once again what he was doing there.

Eugene' first year was particularly hard. Later on, when talking of those days, he used to mention how he found strength from an incident in the life of St Thérèse of Lisieux which reflected something of his own experience. Finding herself on the dimly-lit stairway of her bleak monastery, catching the refrain of music being played in a house across the street, Thérèse thought of the comfort and good cheer of a warm fire on that cold night, contrasting it with the bare floors, unplastered walls and meagre fare of the convent.[91] It seems that Eugene's struggle to persevere in the novitiate became known to friends outside the monastery. Vincent Moloney, writing in the 1960s, remarked that Eugene had told someone – whose name Moloney could no longer remember – 'that, after joining Mount St Joseph, his gay life in Vienna was particularly vivid in his memories. It all came back to him.'[92]

Kevin was fortunate in having Fr Malachy Brasil as his prior and novice master. The moderation and kindness of this priest inspired the young man, and until the end of his life Eugene would

89 Claffey, 'Profiles in Sanctity', pp. 29–30, MSJA.
90 Claffey, 'Profiles in Sanctity', MSJA.
91 Nash, *Catholic Authors*, p.24.
92 Moloney to Fr Nivard, MSJA.

Fr Camillus Claffey with Dom Eugene Boylan at college 1953.

frequently quote him. Fr Brasil was someone who understood him, and to whom he could talk and unburden himself. It was otherwise with Fr Camillus Claffey, who succeeded Fr Brasil in 1933 as prior and master of novice when the latter was elected abbot of Mount St Bernard monastery in Leicestershire in England. Fr Claffey never understood this brilliant young man, felt overawed by him and tended to be defensive in his relations with him.[93] When Eugene was professed with temporary vows at the end of his noviceshsip, he came under the care of Fr Columban Mulcahy (brother of General Richard Mulcahy TD). He was rather military in his exercise of authority, entirely devoted to the monastic ideal, and completely sure of his own vocation. Eugene and he got on well, and Mulcahy was one of the monks who most influenced Eugene.[94]

Before Eugene took his temporary vows and received the black scapular and leather belt of the professed monk, he wrote down a series of resolutions for his future religious life.[95] They reflect the personal fervour of the novice at this important juncture in his life:

1 To see in all that occurs to me, the direct and benevolent hand of God.
2 To hear in every command the voice of God.
3 To let my superiors mould me as they will and how they will.
4 To do all for Mary, with Mary, and in Mary, in union with her Divine Son, that I also may be admitted to her sonship.
5 To remember that in the Office I am part of Our Lord Jesus Christ praising the Father, and that that is the summit of my vocation.
6 In Christ to see, to hear, and be attentive always. This is perhaps the most important of all. (This last resolution was written in German.)

The next day, 11 October 1933, he signed his name 'Mary, Eugene' to the following declaration, expressing his very personal devotion to Mary, the Mother of God:

93 Kinsella, *Dom Eugene Boylan*, p.5.
94 Kinsella, *Dom Eugene Boylan.*
95 Resolutions, 10/10/1931, Notes of Eugene Boylan, MSJ/5/5/2. no.1, MSJA.

> With the help and permission of God, I will do for him,
> through the blessed Virgin Mary, what the Little Flower
> did for the infant Jesus. That is to say, not I but Christ
> upon whom I depend to be 'in me'.[96]

Two days later he wrote to his sister in the Cistercian convent at
Glencairn:

> I find the life here is splendid and my 'niche'. It's not
> exactly easy, knowing me as you do, you can see that,
> but the point is this – there is nothing left for me but to
> become a great saint. I mean there is no use trying to be
> a great philosopher or theologian, or preacher, or director,
> or farmer etc. It simply can't be done here. So you see
> there is only one outlet for surplus energy. Now, about
> this business of becoming a saint. The way is obedience to
> the Rule and prayer, but God's grace is the essential thing.
> Let us pray for it.[97]

The road ahead seemed clear to him, but it would have some
unexpected turns which would challenge Eugene to see anew 'the
direct and benevolent hand of God'.

---

96 Resolutions, MSJA. The 'Little Flower' was a name applied to Marie Thérèse Martin,
who, in religion, took the name Thérèse of the Infant Jesus. She is usually known today
as St Thérèse of Lisieux.

97 Eugene to Magdalen, 13 October 1931, Family Correspondence, MSH 5/5/1.no.8,
MSJA.

CHAPTER 5

ACADEMIC TRAINING AND SPIRITUALITY

Eugene at study in novitiate.

During the second year of his novitiate, Eugene entered on a two-year course in scholastic philosophy, which was followed by three years of theology in preparation for the priesthood. While lectures and study had to be fitted into the already busy schedule of Divine Office and external work, he nevertheless undertook his new studies with characteristic enthusiasm.

CONCERN FOR INTELLECTUAL CLARITY

In later life, Eugene would explain what he most enjoyed in his studies:

> It was not until I commenced philosophy and theology that I began to enjoy serious reading. I can never forget the joy of reading Coffey's *Onthology* and *Epistemology*, where one was in contact with a mind thinking on paper and solving difficulties as they arose. I started theology with the *Summa* of Aquinas, which I read with avidity. Indeed, the style of the theological textbook is the one I relish most, and the succinct clarity of scholastic Latin is a relief from the cultivated obscurity of English philosophical writing. Any urge I have is to condense and summarise. I like to start with a bird's-eye view of the subject and end by seeing things as integrated wholes. So I am quite out of tune with humanistic letters. Beside Aristotle and Aquinas, Homer and Virgil fade into insignificance for me; and only clarity and completeness can make me appreciate any of the modern writers.

On the relevance of his scholastic studies to the Church's apostolate, Eugene observed with characteristic conviction:

> Of two things I am quite convinced. The first is that the most urgent need of the moment is the extension and the intensification of the interior life among all Catholics, and the application of its influence to each and every phase of their activity. The second is that,after the spiritual life, nothing is so necessary as the restoration of metaphysics (in the Aristotelian sense) to its proper place and influence in the intellectual life of Europe and America. I feel no effort should be spared to provide suitable means of training Catholics, especially adult laymen, in the interior life, and of instructing them in philosophy, without unduly interfering with their normal career. There are, of course, many difficulties in

the way of achieving this purpose, but we have to find a way of overcoming them.[98]

DE JAEGHER'S INFLUENCE

The 'interior life' was of the first importance, for it was to it that Eugene had devoted himself. He looked beneath the surface of things, to find the world of spirit, and to find a way to God through getting to know his Son, Jesus Christ, intimately. He was convinced that Jesus lives on in those who are baptised, to such a degree that they constitute a 'mystical body' with him, and are in a special way identified with him. This was central to his belief, and it was a reality that he felt urged to impart to others through his writings.

Eugene's introduction to the life of the spirit and of the heart came from the work of Paul De Jaegher SJ (1880–1958). His book, *One with Jesus* or *The Life of Identification with Christ*, was written originally in French. De Jaegher based his teaching on the Gospels and the writings of St Paul. Following in the tradition of the seventeenth century school of spirituality associated with Cardinal Pierre de Bérulle (1575–1629) and the Jesuit mystical writers – Pierre Lallemant and his disciples Jean Rigoleuc, Jean-Joseph Surin and Julien Maunoir – it proclaimed 'the marvellous doctrine of adherence to Christ, of intimate union with Christ present in the soul, and head of the mystical body.'[99] De Jaegher developed this doctrine in the course of his short book. A significant extract, which would have been well known to Eugene, tells the reader that 'Love for his Father prompted Christ to become man and face death ... He still lives and the immense love of God is carried on by him in his mystical body, in which he continues to glorify his Father ... In order to love the more he has united himself to new individual human natures, to millions of individual human natures, no longer hypostatically, it is true, but still by a very real, intimate and wonderful union'[100] As has been seen, Eugene acknowledged that he was deeply influence by and indebted to De Jaegher' book, which he assimilated

---

98 Hoehn, *Catholic Authors*, pp.38–39.
99 De Jaegher, *One with Jesus*, (London, 1929 ed.), pp.63–64.
100 De Jaegher, *One with Jesus*, pp. 14–15.

and adapted to meet his own needs and those of many others. A distinctive addition was his emphasis on the role of the Mother of God as mother of the members of the mystical body.

Less than a year after his noviciate, one of the first beneficiaries of Boylan's reflections was his sister Kathleen – now Sr Magdalen – in her Cistercian convent.

> Since we can do nothing of ourselves, the one thing necessary is to remain in Christ, as a member of his Mystical Body, completely lost in him. The conditions for that union are the commandments of God, of the Church, of our Rule, of our superiors, and further the will of God as manifested in all that happens to us. To do anything less, or *to do anything more* is to depart from Christ and to embrace death (I may be wrong but that's the way it shows itself to me). And once that is realised Heaven has begun on earth, and the Holy Spirit has given you peace, the depths of which can never be disturbed … It means not initiating anything that Christ does not want. It means, too, that we need no longer rely either on our own good works or our own merits; by our incorporation in Christ, we have His merits, and even if we fail in observing the conditions of membership we have His infinite mercy.

He then went on – perhaps with tongue in cheek, given how individualistic he himself had been – to counsel his sister as follows:

> There's no use in wanting to play the first violin in God's orchestra if you have been made to play the drum, and further you must only wallop your little drum at the right time. If you start improvising you'll ruin the whole symphony.[101]

'LET JESUS BE BORN IN US'

Sometime later, Eugene disclosed that it was only after five years in Roscrea that he came to realise that 'praying meant making love to

101 Eugene to Magdalen, 1 September 1932, MSJA. Italics in text.

Our Lord'. It was only then 'that I began to *pray*', he insisted. 'Our justification, our merits come through our faith and in union with Jesus Christ ... As I see the spiritual life, we come there to get rid of ourselves, to let Jesus be born in us through Mary, and let Him live whatever life suits Him, whether it be a life of joy or suffering, work or calm prayer, whatever He wants it should be all the same to us.'

This was the ideal, but it was very difficult in practice, as his younger sister made clear to him in a letter she wrote a few years later. She had been moved to a convent in France, she did not speak French, and she was feeling quite distressed. Eugene responded in January 1935, unwittingly adopting a paternal role. He brought comfort but strong teaching as well:

> Child dear, when God clearly manifests His will, as He has now, there is only one sensible thing to do, shut off all imagination, all forethought, all consideration and throw your arms around His neck and refuse to look an inch ahead. Our Lord is a most delicate lover. He has foreseen everything – everything. There may be hard things in front of you. He has sent his supply of Grace ahead, *which you won't get until the moment you need it*. He never gives a supply in advance to anyone but beginners ... He has foreseen all your little ways and made provision for them all, not perhaps the provision you would have made ... but then He loves you infinitely more than you do yourself. But He wants your whole heart ... Make a resolution from this moment never to look ahead.

Eugene then advised his sister to 'take it day by day, hour by hour, minute by minute, when desolation becomes intense. It's the only way you can get through the two "Dark Nights" which have to be gone through before you are married to God ... Let Jesus come and live His life in you, and let Him put up with the things He has arranged for ... He must increase, you must decrease.'[102]

These extracts from Eugene's writing, expressed so soon after his

102 Eugene to Magdalen, MSJA. No date except January 1935. Letters to his Sister. Italics in text.

noviciate, anticipate much of the teaching that was later to appeal to thousands of his readers. At this early stage in his monastic journey, he had already acquired a deep understanding of the spiritual life. More challenging, and darker, times lay ahead, however.

FINAL PROFESSION, ORDINATION AND TEACHING

After three years of temporary profession, Eugene was accepted for final profession on 15 October 1936. On 19 May the following year, he was ordained priest. With the permission of the local bishop, the ordination was carried out in the monastic church by Bishop William Lee, an Irishman who was head of the Clifton diocese in England. Eugene's delighted parents and his brother, Gerald, were present. His two sisters and his brother Dermot were unable to attend, because of the strict laws of enclosure laid down in their respective communities.[103]

In later years, Dom Columban Mulcahy was interviewed about his recollections of Eugene during this time, and he had some interesting observations to make. He described Eugene as 'extraordinarily humble, but at the same time very simple and naïve, which shows that his humility did not come natural to him. It was a real supernatural virtue. He could say the most extraordinary things about himself, but he was extremely humble behind it.' He was 'extraordinarily obedient also. He could be childlike in his submission, even though it did not come easily. He was also extraordinary in his recognition of the spiritual qualities of others, even when he didn't ... appreciate their actual qualities.'

Mulcahy saw humility as 'the basic principle' of Eugene's spirituality. Asked if Eugene had any serious crisis before taking solemn vows, he replied, 'No, I don't think so. I don't think he ever seriously questioned his vocation. He had a lot of difficulties. For example, Dom Camillus, looking after the novices (and who became abbot at a later stage) would pick him up on small points in his sermons, in his writings etc., which could be very aggravating, but Eugene never seriously doubted his vocation.' When asked if

103 Claffey, 'Profiles in Sanctity', p. 30, MSJA.

Eugene's spirituality was truly monastic, or if he generalised too much from his own experience, Mulcahy was definite in his reply: 'I think his experience as a layman coloured his monastic spirituality, but he accepted wholeheartedly the fundamental monastic principles.' What of his devotion to the Blessed Virgin Mary? Was it perhaps unbalanced? Mulcahy thought not. 'Eugene was always probing the theological foundations of the devotion. There was nothing overdone about it. He certainly believed that every legitimate honour should be given to Our Lady.'

When asked whether Eugene's spirituality was more or less formed before entering Roscrea, Mulcahy's response was revealing: 'He hardly had the theological side of it formed. He begged me to use influence to stop his being sent to the college before ordination so that he could really concentrate on his theological formation. He read the *Summa* on his own very consistently.'[104] This last response raises an issue that would subsequently cause Eugene much pain: his reluctance to get involved in teaching in the boarding school attached to the Abbey. In September 1937, a few months after his ordination, at the urgent request of the college authorities, Eugene was appointed to teach in the college.[105] He was less than enthusiastic about this appointment, however, and would later view his reluctance as a failure in obedience and the beginning of a period of spiritual trial and psychological strain.

In the 1930s, from 1932–1938, the community at Mount St Joseph could not avoid learning of the hardships being experienced by people in the locality as a result of an economic war between the Irish and British governments. The Irish government, under Éamon de Valera, refused to pay land annuities to Britain. In retaliation, the British government imposed a twenty per cent duty on two-thirds of Irish exports to the United Kingdom. The depressing effect of this was severe on communities of low- and middle-income farmers, with the value of cattle dropping to unprecedented levels. In the diocese of Killaloe, where the monastery was situated, the impact

---

104 'Interviews', Nivard interviewing Mulcahy at Nunraw Abbey, Scotland, MSJA.
105 Claffey, 'Profiles in Sanctity', p. 30, MSJA.

was such that the redoubtable Bishop Michael Fogarty launched a bitter public attack on the Irish government and its policies. The climate of criticism was reinforced by the divisions of the recent Irish Civil War (1922–23), and the controversy inevitably found echoes among the teaching staff of the monastery's college.

It appears that Eugene, as a member of the teaching staff, became caught up in the divisive and critical atmosphere of the time. As a consequence, his inner serenity and his ease in prayer were disturbed, and he lost his feeling of closeness to God. Many years later, Eugene spoke about this experience to Fr Paschal, a fellow religious in the monastery of Caldey in Wales. As recalled by Paschal, Eugene told him that once, as a young professed monk,

> he received mystical graces, and was introduced to the prayer of quietude. Then this happens, he was appointed as teacher at the Abbey school, and he did not accept it wholeheartedly; and he did emphasise that point: his obedience was not complete … From that time onwards, his mystical life stopped and … he said he never went further, and it never came again … and he gave me the reason for it … 'When appointed a teacher, I found myself involved with the other teachers; and at that time there was among them an unhealthy spirit of criticism. I gave in myself, and that was the end of my mystical graces for me.'[106]

The fact that he was not a successful teacher of boys only added to Eugene's problems. One forthright colleague stated bluntly that he was 'a disaster as a teacher, so bad that his classes were unable to do the public examinations'.[107] It wasn't that the boys disliked him; in fact it appears that he was popular with them. They knew of his academic work in Vienna, were somewhat in awe of him, and enjoyed eliciting from him stories of his time in the Austrian capital.

---

106 Fr Paschal, Caldey Island, Wales, MSJ/5/5/3 no.1, MSJA. Notes concerning Eugene, memoirs/histories.
107 Interviews with Cistercian colleagues of Eugene Boylan, conducted by Dr Louise O'Reilly on 5 June 2013. [Hereafter, MSJ Interviews by L. O'R]

The problem was with his style of teaching. He tended to use a lecture mode in the classroom instead of stooping to the level of his young students in his teaching.

For Eugene ordination meant, in the first place, the privilege of celebrating Mass. It meant participating in the mysterious power coming from the Holy Spirit through the ministry of the Church, whereby the bread and wine, transformed into the body and blood of Christ, would be given as food for believers in their life's journey. He was in awe of the gift of the priesthood, and always conducted his Mass with devotion and dignity.

He also had a deep awareness of the further gift he had received through his ordination, the gift of bringing absolution and comfort to all who came to him for the sacrament of penance. As confessor, Eugene brought with him his personal humility, a deep empathy towards those seeking absolution and counsel, and a spirit of consolation. He became widely popular as a confessor, not only in the surrounding locality but, most significantly, among many of his fellow monks who chose him as their confessor.

Shortly after ordination, Eugene received faculties to preach to the congregations who came to Mass in the monastery church on Sundays, and he soon won acclaim as a preacher. Soon, requests began to arrive inviting him to preach at special celebrations and to direct retreats.[108]

THE DEATH OF HIS FATHER

The Boylan family, so joyous at Eugene's ordination, experienced the harshness of life a short time later when Eugene's father, Richard, suffered a serious decline in health. As Easter 1939 approached, he was in such a poor condition that Eugene was sent to visit him. Writing of the visit to one of her daughters, Eugene's mother Agnes – referring to her husband as 'Dick' or 'D' – recalled Eugene's visit.

> He left on 8 o'clock p.m. train on Sunday night and near midnight I heard the old '3 rings'! Great joy. He was like a breath of sunshine in the house. Wore his habit and

108 Claffey, 'Profiles in Sanctity', p. 31, MSJA.

danced around, and the piano was well exercised. He was rather shocked at Papa's appearance, but on Easter Monday Papa was like a new man. He walked round the garden and that day was like old times ... I was afraid D. would be done out, but he got his first good night's sleep and on Tuesday morning he was anointed. It was a really beautiful and touching ceremony. Fr D ... with a lovely pleated surplice, Kevin in his robes at the foot of the bed and myself. The sun is streaming in (our bedroom ... looks out on the garden) and all was such peace. Soon after, Dick was calling for something to eat! He got up and had a day of ease from pain. I felt like a three-year-old with happiness. On Wednesday morning Kevin brought him Holy Viaticum again (Fr D. having heard his confession). Kevin says he never saw even a religious with such a perfect disposition ... Kevin told him that perhaps his vocation was to suffer in the front line and it looks like it. Kevin was hardly gone when he got worse ... He had a bad night and is in pain all day.

This harrowing letter was followed, on 3 May, with another one, containing the news that the doctor had diagnosed incurable cancer. Agnes wrote that the doctor thought her husband might last several months, as his heart was strong, but that he would grow progressively weaker. She had not told her husband, who wanted her nearby, that he was dying. 'He can only walk an inch at a time with two sticks,' she wrote. 'He would not take morphia for me. (He is) afraid of forming a habit and would like to *bear his pain as long as possible.*' [109]

When his father died some months later, Eugene was present to bring comfort to his mother and to his brother, Gerald, the only other member of the family able to be present. Gerald looked after the funeral and other immediate arrangements, and remained a focal point of support and contact for all the family. Being a resilient woman, Agnes endeavoured after he husband's death to expand her music practice in order to obtain financial security. She kept herself

109 Idem, 3 May 1939.

active, and found occasion to visit Roscrea, sometimes staying over in the guest house and becoming a familiar figure to the monks. Eugene kept up a regular correspondence with her that was marked by a mixture of spirituality, affection and fun.

NEW ROLE, NEW DIRECTIONS
During this time, Eugene continued to experience dryness in his spiritual life. The monastic life had tended to become a monotonous treadmill, and he felt as if God had abandoned him.[110] He had matured spiritually, however, since the Clonliffe years, and he had learned much from his wide reading and reflection. There was no question of giving up his way of life. He soldiered on from day to day, leaving himself in God's hands.

Fortunately for him, his way was eased by his being removed from the Abbey school. He was given the more congenial role of 'Master of Scholastics', which included teaching philosophy and subsequently moral and dogmatic theology, to the younger monks.[111] He brought enthusiasm to the task, and made full use of the voice and speaking skills that had so impressed those present at the L & H meetings. He was successful in his new role, and his enthusiasm 'passed on to at least some of his students'.[112] He was described as bringing a 'fresh outlook'.[113]

At the same time he was appointed to hear confessions in the public church attached to the monastery. Frequent confession was the norm at the time, and four priests were regularly employed hearing confessions. Eugene quickly gained a reputation for kindness and understanding. He brought to his role as confessor a wider experience of lay life than most of his fellow monks and, backed by his extensive reading and in-depth study, he conveyed assurance in his judgements. As Fr Nivard noted:

He had two outstanding charisms. He could meet any

---

110 From his article in *Doctrine and Life*, which appears to reflect his personal experience, p. 289.
111 Claffey, 'Profiles in Sanctity', p. 30, MSJA. Kinsella, *Dom Eugene Boylan*, p.7.
112 Kinsella, *Dom Eugene Boylan*.
113 MSJ Interviews by L. O'R, p. 4.

account of a situation or a problem with a sympathy that
was totally non-judgemental and that inspired enormous
confidence ... He had great common sense and brought
this to bear on any problem. He had profound sympathy
for the weaknesses of human nature, and while he was
quite clear in his mind where right and wrong lay, he never
condemned anyone and never turned anyone away.[114]

Some years later, when asked in Australia to give a conference to
priests on confessional practice and spiritual direction, Eugene's
emphasis was unmistakable. 'Do not judge people, never express
surprise at anything, realise your own weakness and sinfulness, and
your own need of mercy; and above all, keep your mouth shut unless
you see some positive good to be done by talking.'[115] Not surprisingly,
demand for Fr Boylan as a confessor grew among all sections of
the Catholic population, diocesan priests and religious as well the
laity. It was a time when many people were crippled with scruples,
mortal sin seemed everywhere and hell loomed threateningly. In
the midst of much fear, Eugene assured people of God's mercy and
understanding.

Requests had begun to come from religious groups for him to
conduct days of spiritual conferences and to give longer retreats.
By the early 1940s, through these events, he had become aware of
people's widespread interest in prayer, and the evident need of priests
and religious for help in this area of their lives. Many of them, he
came to see, had inadequate, even harmful, ideas of God and of
prayer, and he felt called to meet their needs. It seems that the final
impetus to write came during a retreat he gave to the Irish Christian
Brothers at which he was asked to write a book on prayer.[116]

---

114 Kinsella, *Dom Eugene Boylan*, p. 7.
115 Kinsella, *Dom Eugene Boylan*, p. 8.
116 Abbot Columba Mulcahy, interviewed by Fr Nivard, MSJA.

CHAPTER 6

INTERNATIONAL ACCLAIM

Eugene Boylan's first book, *Difficulties in Mental Prayer*, which appeared in 1943, made his reputation as a writer and spiritual director. It merits close attention. Despite the title, it was not primarily concerned with difficulties in mental prayer as such; rather it was aimed at helping Christians to seek spiritual perfection. It was mainly addressed to people in religious congregations and to diocesan clergy, but it also had lay readers in mind. It was written at the request of Br Luke Ryan who, together with some other Irish Christian Brothers, was on retreat at the monastery guest house in Roscrea.[117]

THE CENTRALITY OF PRAYER AND SPIRITUAL READING

The essential requirements for spiritual perfection, the author insists, are prayer and spiritual reading. He follows the standard description of prayer as 'an elevation of the mind and heart to God, to adore Him, to praise Him, to thank Him for His benefits and to beg His grace and mercy'.[118] To prepare oneself for prayer, it is necessary to condition one's mind and spirit by meditating on matters that raise the mind and heart to God. Spiritual reading serves the same purpose. It should be preceded by asking the guidance of the Holy Spirit, and should be conducted in a reflective manner. Meditation and spiritual reading, Eugene insists, are but a prelude to prayer. They are not prayer itself. They serve to give rise to 'affections' in prayer by which the soul 'moves towards God' in words or in silence. Using a scholastic approach, Boylan talks about 'the powers of the soul': the role played in prayer by intellect and will, imagination and memory, as well as the external senses. He mentions the function of each, while pointing out that it is through the will alone that sin can be committed. He speaks of practical methods of prayer that

117 Claffey, 'Profiles in Sanctity', p. 27, MSJA.
118 E. Boylan. *Difficulties in Mental Prayer* (Manila ed. 1985), p. 2. The book was published in 1943, but the edition followed here is the 1985 edition.

everyone might employ, and of different stages of prayer that may arise in the individual's life. He acknowledges that for many people prayer is very difficult. It is sometimes an arid experience, when there is no sense of a relationship with God. Some give up prayer as a result, while others consult books of meditation seeking a method that will enable them to feel close to God.

Eugene goes on to point out that, in reality, there are as many reasons for difficulties in prayer as there are people wishing to pray. Each one is different. Frequently, however, problems arise from people's idea of God. For many, he points out, God is still a severe, distant, judgemental figure, taking note of one's faults and weaknesses. With such a God, any sense of a trusting relationship is almost impossible. Eugene's emphasis is on God as a loving father, the 'Abba-Father' of St Paul, whose mercy and empathy are portrayed in Jesus Christ.

In the monastic tradition the spirit of prayer extends throughout the day. In the more publicly active religious orders, and in the case of the diocesan clergy, it is necessary to set aside times for mental prayer. Such arrangements can often be compromised by pressure of work, Eugene notes, and in that situation it is essential that spiritual reading be maintained. If time for even that fails during the week, efforts must be made to find time at weekends. As a general rule, Eugene insists, 'to reduce the time for spiritual reading, without due cause, to less than three hours a week is to starve the soul and bring about the consequences of such starvation'.[119]

Eugene notes that reading and meditation are only reading and thinking about God, while prayer is 'talking to God', a conversation which may develop into 'looking at God and loving Him'.[120] Summarising the purpose of his book, and quoting St John of the Cross and St Teresa of Ávila, he points out that religious life, in essence, is a state of tending to perfection, and that it is 'impossible to tend properly and completely to perfection without leading an interior life'. In the absence of an interior life 'it is impossible for a

119 Boylan, *Difficulties in Mental Prayer*, p. 16.
120 Boylan, *Difficulties in Mental Prayer*, p. 18.

priest or religious to live an exterior life that is not ruined by sterility, supernatural uselessness and inefficiency'.[121]

UNION WITH CHRIST

Eugene contends that for many people – religious, clergy and laity – the root of the problem lies in the fact that we do not have 'a lively practical faith in the effects of baptism and the possibilities of the Christian life. We do not realise that the Christian life is the life of Christ lived by Christ in us, not merely our own paltry existence, dragged out in lonely weakness ... If the sacraments effect what they signify ... what conclusion may be drawn from the fact that in the Sacrament of the Blessed Eucharist the Body and Blood of Christ is given to us for our *food?* – What limit may we set to the strength or to the possibility of the soul which is nourished by the living flesh of God Himself?'[122]

In the context of the Blessed Eucharist, Boylan emphasises the special partnership of the priest with Christ. 'The priest's union with the Lord is so close that he consecrates and absolves in the first person – "This is *my* Body"; '*I* absolve you".' For the priest, then, 'a true conviction of his own powerlessness and his constant need for help' will soon lead him 'to a vivid sense of partnership with Jesus.'[123] Eugene devotes a special chapter to the clergy, giving advice and encouragement to them about seeking perfection and gaining a close union with Christ. He emphasises that 'holiness is a primary duty, and a practical possibility'.

In his emphasis on Christ's interest in and love for each person, Boylan at times gets carried away on wings of rhetorical fervour; this would happen again in *This Tremendous Lover*. For example, he writes, 'Every single Christian soul can say: "During every moment of His life Jesus thought of *me*, and loved *me*; in all His sufferings He had *my* needs in His mind, and in His view; in all His joys, His Heart was set on sharing these joys with *me*".'[124] There is no evidence

121 Boylan, *Difficulties in Mental Prayer*, pp. 119–20.
122 Boylan, *Difficulties in Mental Prayer*, p. 121.
123 Boylan, *Difficulties in Mental Prayer*, pp. 69–70.
124 Boylan, *Difficulties in Mental Prayer*, pp. 122–3, on how he prayed.

for such statements in the New Testament, and indeed if they were true, Jesus would not have been truly human. But he was. We are told that Jesus was like us in all things but sin (Heb. 4:15). The evangelists testify to his fear and horror at the death he would have to undergo. They tell us how he prayed to be spared the crucifixion, and how he felt abandoned by his Father. The reality we read about in Scripture is far from the notion that in the midst of all Jesus' suffering he was thinking personally of each of the millions of individual Christians who would live for the next two thousand years.

The type of oratorical piety enunciated here by Eugene was in widespread use during much of the nineteenth and well into the twentieth century. Its preachers had little sense of the historical Jesus, and did not advert to the fact that they were in effect minimising the reality of the Incarnation. Eugene, despite his scientific training and extensive reading, manifested little awareness of the historical scholarship that had recently led to major developments in the study of Scripture. Already in 1942, Pope Pius XII had issued his encyclical *Divino afflante Spiritu,* which represented a major milestone in Catholic scripture study. Eugene's approach to the gospel narratives remained unaffected by these developments. Significantly, the Gospel he mainly used was that of St John. He based most of his spirituality on the letters of St Paul.[125]

Despite this occasional excess in presentation and the contemporary habit of speaking of people as 'souls', nothing can hide Eugene's real desire for God and his wish that others might find the Lord in prayer. He is convinced that each one must resolve never to give up his attempt to progress in prayer.

> Let him take up prayer ... as a quest for Jesus, a striving
> for close union with Jesus ... Let him proceed to pray to
> Our Lord in his own words as soon as he can and as often
> as he can. Let him not be afraid to talk to God without
> words whenever he can ... Let him throughout the day

125 Kinsella, *Dom Eugene Boylan,* p. 9. Much of Eugene's theology came from two works: Fernand Prat SJ, *The Theology of St Paul,* 2 vols., (London: Burns, Oates & Washbourne, 1938); and Emile Mersch SJ, *The Whole Christ. The Theology of the Mystical Body,* (The Bruce Pub. Co., 1938)..

make frequent aspirations to Jesus; they should not be long, they need not be verbal; a sigh or a smile of the heart is sufficient. Let him seek Jesus in all things; let him unite himself to Jesus by doing what pleases Him – by doing the will of God. That is the way to lay hold of Jesus.[126]

Then, echoing his own experience and that of many others, Eugene adds, 'If all power of prayer seems to be lost, if the time of prayer becomes a period of abstractions and aridity, let him not lose courage, nor change his resolution. His prayer then is made by submitting to the will of God as completely and as generously as he can.' In such circumstances, Eugene adds, many people get great help by using a book, but he warns once again of the danger of turning prayer into spiritual reading. The reader must stop frequently, turning his heart to God and listening to whatever God may have to say to him. 'Perseverance under this heavy trial has a great reward and touches the heart of God.'[127]

Keeping in mind the problem of suffering in people's lives, Eugene observes that one 'should try to be ready to accept any suffering that God sends him, for union with Jesus is sealed in the fellowship of his sufferings, and by our patient endurance we are made partakers of the passion of Christ. But our aim must be humility. The Kingdom of God is already within us, but we make it our own by our poverty of spirit. This is our title to union with God, and it is the first principle of the spiritual life that Our Lord taught in public.'[128]

Finally, Eugene insists that one 'must never, never trust in oneself and, above all, one must never, never, under any circumstances, cease to trust Jesus absolutely; God became man to save sinners, to give life to those who are dead in sin, to give strength to the weak and weary, to give Himself to the humble, to the poor in spirit. Let us take Him at His word.'[129]

Difficulties in Mental Prayer rapidly became very popular in Catholic circles including, to Eugene's surprise, among the laity. 'I

126 Boylan, *Difficulties in Mental Prayer*, p. 121.
127 Boylan, *Difficulties in Mental Prayer*, p. 125.
128 Boylan, *Difficulties in Mental Prayer*, p. 125.
129 Boylan, *Difficulties in Mental Prayer* p. 126.

wouldn't have expected the Mental Prayer book to have much appeal outside convents etc.', he wrote subsequently. 'There's a publisher pressing me for a book on the Spiritual Life for *Laity*! But I don't get enough time – and I wonder how much do I know about the problems of the laity.'[130]

Difficulties in Mental Prayer appealed greatly to priests and religious. Eugene's sister, Molly, wrote from her convent in Cincinnatti in 1961:[131]

> Your books are continually being recommended by priests. One Maryknoll Father who said Mass here recently said that the Father General gave each priest a copy of *Difficulties in Mental Prayer* for ordination. I do hope you may be able to do some more writing as in this way you reach so very many souls.

The book was used widely in novitiates and seminaries not only in Ireland, but throughout the English-speaking world. It was translated into all the main European languages and, forty-five years after its publication, it was reissued in the US and the Philippines. Despite the extensive literature on prayer published in the last forty years and the changing world of spirituality, *Difficulties in Mental Prayer* continues to be helpful to many people seeking spiritual perfection.

A PROFUSION OF PUBLICATIONS

In later years, Eugene wrote a number of books in a rather similar genre. These were *The Spiritual Life of the Priest (1949), The Priest's Way to God* (1961) and *Partnership with Christ* (1964). All of these sold well, as did an earlier book entitled *The Mystical Body* (1948). Extant letters to the author indicated how helpful these books were to many people.

Before all of these works were written, sometime in the 1930s, Eugene had written a short biography of a young French monk, Michel Carlier, who had been a member of the Cistercian monastery

130 Eugene to Aileen O'Connell, Dublin, 9 October 1944, MSJ 5/5/1, no. 11, file 1, MSJA.
131 Molly to Eugene, 5 February 1961, MSJ 5/5/1 no.6, MSJA.

of Chimay in Belgium. Conscripted in 1914, Carlier distinguished himself in the war and was killed by a shell in 1917. 'I aspire to one thing only,' Carlier had written, 'to do whatever the good God wishes from me, however uninviting it may be'. As Eugene commented, 'The essence of sanctity could hardly be formulated more excellently'. Publication of this book, under the title *A Mystic Under Arms*, was delayed until 1945.[132]

A year later, 1946, Eugene's's magnum opus appeared. *This Tremendous Lover* was to prove one of the most successful spiritual books of the twentieth century. It made Eugene Boylan's name a familiar one across the English-speaking world and well beyond. The following year, *The Mystical Body* and *The Spiritual Life* appeared in a notable burst of energy and creativity. It was remarkable that he published these three books in quick succession, but more remarkable still was the fact that he was able to write at all in a monastic environment that accounted for most hours of the day and was not adapted to producing works for publication.

To get the manuscript of *Difficulties in Mental Prayer* typed Eugene had to enlist the help of his mother. He then had to send the typed copy to the official censor, whose function was to ensure that it contained nothing heretical or unacceptable to the order. When passed by the censor, the decision about a publisher rested with the prior.[133] To find time to write at all was a basic problem.

'As a Cistercian', he said, 'writing is a spare-time job, and a Cistercian has no spare time. The Divine Office takes six hours a day,' not to mention the daily manual work and other community duties and chores. Eugene found it hard to write to a schedule, 'and the whole monastic life is a schedule.'[134]

To find time to write, he stole hours from his sleep at night. The favourable reception of *Difficulties in Mental Prayer*, by lay people in particular, spurred him on to write *This Tremendous Lover*, for it was his conviction that 'the most urgent need of the moment is the

132 For information on this book, I am indebted to Fr Laurence Walsh OCSO, Mount St Joseph Abbey, Roscrea.
133 Eugene to his mother, 18 November 19, MSJA.
134 Hoehn, *Catholic Authors*, p. 38.

extension and the intensification of the interior spiritual life among all Catholics, and the application of its influence to each and every phase of their activity'.[135]

THIS TREMENDOUS LOVER

The publisher of this book, the much-respected Captain John Feehan of Mercier Press, advised authors of spiritual books to 'write only from experience, if one tries to write in what he has not experienced, it will be seen through … People are not fooled. A writer must give a true account of his journey. Readers of a spiritual book can at once discern any hint of complacency or falsity in the author's experience.' It is part of the strength of Eugene's *This Tremendous Lover* that it carries an earnestness and conviction that gives power to his words. By repeating an idea or image in slightly different forms, he communicates like a rhetorician, and the result can be very effective. This method is already evident in both the preface and the introduction he wrote, as he endeavours to explain the purpose of the book. Early in the preface, he states succinctly:

> This book is an attempt to outline the love story of God and man … and to show that the spiritual life is a partnership of love between God and man which can be summed up in one word – Christ. Instead of describing a *mere* union of companionship, we have attempted to use St Paul's concept of an organic unity in one body – in one Christ … To foster the development of that union with God in the lives of the faithful is the purpose of this book.[136]

Conscious of the need to emphasise the nature of our human love for God, and to avoid any misunderstanding arising from some contemporary schools of psychology, Eugene insists:

> The love of man for God presupposes a new nature, a sharing of the divine nature, an elevation of the whole being of man to a new order by grace … It would be a grievous error to conceive the love of God as anything

135 Hoehn. *Catholic Authors*, p. 39.
136 Eugene Boylan, *This Tremendous Lover*, (Dublin: The Mercier Press, 1946), pp, viii, X.

which essentially involves sense emotion or feeling. The love of God lies in the grace-aided will ... A very high degree of love of God is quite compatible with an absence of any feeling of emotion, and even with the presence of a feeling of distaste for the service of God ... Love is the conformity of our will to the will of God.[137]

Starting from the principle of our incorporation in Christ and our vocation to the everlasting union with him in heaven, Eugene claims that this leads to 'a practical programme of humility (accepting oneself with all one's deficiencies), charity (one adjusts oneself to other members of society and lives for them as well as for oneself), and abandonment (fulfilling one's allotted task and accepting willingly all that Providence allows to happen in one's life)'. Without apology, Eugene asserts that

the summit of divine love is proposed to everybody. Such a height must be reached here or hereafter. There is no choice finally except heaven or hell. Heaven supposes perfect love of God and must either be reached in this life, or else with far more suffering in the next life through the fires of purgatory. The easier way is to be sanctified here and now ... What we regard as essential is that the soul should put itself in daily contact with Our Lord; and what we suggest in this book is an outline of the way to achieve that end and to make the daily contact a fruitful one. If that much is done, we feel the rest can be safely left to the guidance of Our Lord.

Turning once again to the purpose of the work, Eugene declares that the book considers 'the importance of the interior life for the individual Christian'. This is important for the Catholic body as a whole, he claims. 'The only hope for civilisation in its present crisis is that Catholics succeed in leavening society. Their success in doing so depends primarily not on their organisation but on their interior life and personal love of God.' He asserts that Catholic Action without an interior life will effect very little: 'If we Catholics have not had

137 Boylan, *This Tremendous Lover*, pp.xi, xii.

the influence on society that our numbers should have produced the reason is to be found in our own lack of interior life.'[138] There is a shortcut to union with Christ, Boylan asserts, for the individual and for society; it is through Our Lady, who brought Christ into the world and is still doing so.

In the introduction, Eugene returns again, but this time at greater length, to the purpose of the book:

> The purpose of these pages is to show what Our Lord's plan for our happiness is and to indicate how we are to co-operate in its achievement. What is written in this book is addressed to every Christian, especially those who have come to feel the limitations of their own human self, and who feel the need of something more than their own unaided efforts can achieve. For this book is the story of a partnership – a partnership between God and the human soul, which happens at baptism – a partnership which should, by the joint action of both partners lead to an ecstasy of perpetual union in heaven. To perform one's own share of the work, one must have knowledge ... for knowledge must come before love.

For this reason, many pages of the book 'are given to an attempt to show the fundamental unity and connection of God's plan', for 'once one has caught a glimpse of the meaning of God's plan to restore all things in Christ, one has the key, not only to the whole history of the universe, but also to the history and destiny of one's own soul. All the details of the spiritual life fall into their proper perspective, and the quest of perfection is seen to be both possible and reasonable for every Christian.'[139]

Eugene's attempt to outline God's plan runs to twenty-four chapters, starting with 'The Beginning and the Fall', and continuing with chapter headings such as 'Redemption', 'The Mystical Body of Christ', 'Partnership with Christ', 'Seeking Christ through Humility and Obedience', 'Seeking Christ in Prayer', 'Seeking Christ by

138 Boylan, *This Tremendous Lover*, pp. xiii, xiv.
139 Boylan, *This Tremendous Lover*, Introduction, pp. xviii–xix.

Reading', 'Conversation with Christ', 'Christ in His Sacraments', 'Christ, Our Food and Our Life', 'Union with Christ through Abandonment', 'Union with Christ in Our Neighbour', 'Union with Christ through Humility', 'Christ's Life-Giving Cross', 'Confidence in Christ', 'Marriage and Holiness', 'Mary, the Mother of the Whole Christ', 'Christ, Our Tremendous Lover', and 'One Christ Loving Himself.'

THE BOOK'S RECEPTION

This Tremendous Lover was very well received by reviewers. Already by November of 1946, Eugene wrote to a friend, 'Sales good, 1,500 gone in the first week and orders coming in'.[140] It soon became evident that the book was having an influence on many readers, something Eugene became aware of through the correspondence he received in the years following publication. One woman wrote, 'The most important thing for me is that you know the powerful effect your book has had upon me and how much I have fallen in love with it and your words.'[141] Another reader reported, 'The effects of your books on my life can only be attributed to your life of prayer and sacrifice. You sow while I reap'.[142] One religious commented, 'I cannot say how much good it has done me, and I go back to it again and again. It's difficult to say which chapter helps me most, but I find that on "Humility" a great comfort and consolation.'[143] Another writer informed Eugene that he had read a newspaper report stating that Princess Margaret (of the British Royal Family), on a visit to Ireland, 'expressed a wish to visit one of her favourite spiritual writers – you!'[144] From America, the Franciscan Friar, Florence F. Hoste of St Leonard's College, Ohio, wrote to Eugene, 'I have profited much from the reading of your books ... In dealing with lay people seeking perfection, I have found *This Tremendous Lover*

140 Eugene to Billy Kingston, 12 November 1946, MSJ 5/5/1 no. 14, MSJA.
141 Mrs Arthur C. Trebnes to Eugene, 24 November 1959, MSJ. 5/5/1, no.14, file 1, MSJA.
142 Correspondence to Eugene, unsigned, undated, MSJA.
143 Sr. M. Patrick, Convent of Mercy, Clara, Co. Offaly to Eugene, 28 December 1960, MSJ 5/5/1 no. 12, MSJA.
144 Fr John Carroll, SSJ to Eugene, 1 June 1961, MSJ. 5/5/1 no.12, MSJA.

very helpful. [It] inspired me to initiate a movement to teach mental prayer to the laity.'[145]

This success was both gratifying and disturbing for Eugene. It led to an overwhelming demand for him to conduct retreats and give lectures. On 12 February 1961, he wrote to his abbot, Camillus Claffey, following a retreat at the Cistercian monastery of Nunraw, Scotland, 'I find myself taking up a very definite line on spirituality and speaking with certainty even authority. Yet the contrast between what I teach and what I am makes me wonder if there isn't a mistake somewhere'.[146]

One person who had no misgivings about the success of the book was Captain John Feehan of Mercier Press. Looking back on his time working with Eugene, he recalled that it was 'one of the most productive and satisfying periods of my entire career as a publisher. At intervals of about a month or so I visited the monastery and went through each chapter with him as he had written it. Sometimes he adopted my ideas and criticism, sometimes he rejected them. After 18 months the manuscript was completed, and a few months later, published. That was 20 years ago, and it is as alive today as it was in those first years. Vatican II has not only not made it out of date, but on the contrary has enhanced its message.'[147]

As regards Feehan's claim that the book is consonant with the Second Vatican Council, two points can be made. First of all, the Second Vatican Council, in its emphasis on ecumenism, gave considerably less attention to the role of Our Lady than did Eugene, writing almost twenty years earlier. Secondly, Eugene's almost exclusive emphasis on the crucifixion in the redemption of humankind is very much of its time. The Second Vatican Council, in addition to the crucifixion, stressed also the centrality of the resurrection, viewing the death and resurrection of Jesus as two facets of a single saving event. As scripture scholar and theologian, David Stanley, writing during the Second Vatican Council put it, 'Our

145 Hoste to Eugene, 20 June 1960, MSJ 5/5/1 no.14, file 1, MSJA.
146 Eugene to Claffey, re retreat at Nunraw, 12 Feb. 1961, MSJ 5/5/1 no. 16, MSJA.
147 Capt. John Feehan in *A Publisher and his World* (Dublin: Mercier Press, 1969), MSJ 5/5/1. no.14 file 1, MSJA.

Lord's death, resurrection, ascension, exaltation, and his sending of the Holy Spirit, while separate in our time-space, constitute a unique saving event, the principal object of the Christian faith'.[148] At the time when Eugene was writing *This Tremendous Lover*, the resurrection of Christ had not yet received the attention in theology or in popular devotion which it subsequently received.

Despite these differences in emphasis, Feehan's claim that the Second Vatican Council had not made *This Tremendous Lover* out of date is confirmed by the fact that, sixty years after its publication, it is still being reprinted and has been made available in many languages throughout the world. It can be found on Amazon with a five-star rating as 'The Beloved Spiritual Classic on God's Pursuit of the Soul'. A 'Catholic Review' by Julie Davis (2012) asserts, 'This is one of the most practical, down-to-earth books I have ever read about living one's Catholic faith in everyday life'. On 27 June 2015, a male commentator observed, 'To me this was a transformative book. It answered some questions I had for years and created a path for me to enhance and strengthen my prayer life.' No doubt, Eugene would have been overjoyed and humbled by the words of an American woman reader in January 2016, who enthused, 'This is a great book. It will transform Jesus into someone who loves you. When I go to Mass, I see Jesus in a new way, and I love Him that much more. He is the Tremendous Lover. He loves us all deeply.'

As his renown spread, Eugene received requests from many journals – including *Doctrine and Life* and *The Furrow* in Ireland, *The Clergy Review* in Britain and *Ave Maria* in the US – to write articles for their publications. These articles reached a very wide audience across the English-speaking world, and Eugene received many appreciative responses, such as this one from the US: 'Thank you for your "Partnership with Christ" series ... they are the most inspiring articles I have ever read ... Without reservation, it has been impossible not to buy *Ave Maria*.'[149]Another reader wrote

---

148 D. Stanley SJ, *A Modern Scriptural Approach to the Spiritual Exercises* (The Institute of Jesuit Sources, 1966), pp. 275–6.

149 Rosamund Collis, Mass. USA to Eugene, MSJ 5/5/1 no.14, file 3, MSJA, undated.

of an article 'Confidence in God', also published in *Ave Maria*, 'I'd like to see your message shouted from the housetops to our fear-bound world. I feel people try to lose themselves in worldly pleasures because they are afraid to hope. They have been hurt and disappointed so often.'[150]

'Partnership with Christ', a series of articles published in *Ave Maria*, was made available as a book in the spring of 1964. Earlier, a collection of articles written for the American monthly, *The Priest*, formed the basis for Eugene's *The Spiritual Life of the Priest*, published by Mercier Press in 1949. In his short introduction to this book, Eugene speaks of diocesan priests 'whose vocation we consider to be one of the most difficult of all'. His time in Clonliffe had given him a special empathy with the diocesan priest and his work, and it's not surprising that many clergy came to him for confession and spiritual advice.

At the start of his life as a Cistercian monk, Eugene spoke of finding his 'niche'. As teacher in the abbey school, he found himself in a role to which he was unsuited. Now, as writer, lecturer and retreat-giver, he had found an outlet that was spiritually enriching for others and satisfying to himself in his vocation. It was a 'niche' within the community 'niche'. His writing, as has been seen, had to be accomplished within the confines of the community timetable and was subject always to obedience. Similarly, the numerous requests for retreats and conferences, following his literary success, came up against the problem of his vow of stability, which required special permission for him to go outside the monastery. Although he and the abbot did not relate easily to each other, Eugene appears to have been punctilious in his observance of obedience as regards both his writing and his outside activities.

The next period in his life would arise directly because of obedience. He was instructed to travel to Australia to make a Cistercian foundation there. He would find that his writings had gone before him, and would influence the people he met.

150 Mar. D. Maheu to Eugene, 4 Oct. 1961, MSJ 5/5/1 no.11, file 3, MSJA.

CHAPTER 7

PLANNING A NEW FOUNDATION IN AUSTRALIA, 1953–55

During Eugene's initial period in Roscrea, from 1931 to 1953, the world and Ireland had undergone immense change. On the world stage, Nazi Germany and Soviet Communism had become dominant forces, and the ambitions of both paved the way for the Second World War (1939–45). In Ireland, from 1932 to 1948, the prevailing government party was Fianna Fáil led by Éamon de Valera. The de Valera government survived the 'economic war', gained the return of Irish ports that had been in British hands, and maintained a position of neutrality during the Second World War. Life in Ireland during the war years was austere if largely secluded from the horrors of the war. The monastery in Roscrea was self-sufficient in terms of food, but received little news of the outside world. Such news as they received came from the contacts of the guestmaster, or from those teaching in the school, or from letters.

On 30 May 1940, Eugene comforted his mother with a letter referring to her son Dermot, then in England. 'Dermot is in a bad place – as far as air raids go – still nothing will happen to him that God does not intend, so he's all right.' He added, 'The little news that seeps in here is bad. Perhaps I'm wrong, but God's dealings with France have been extraordinary – and the conversion of France is the one hope of Catholicity in Europe, as I see it.' He then reassured his mother about his sister Magdalen's move to a Cork convent. 'M need have no anxiety about Cork, unless the IRA gets out of hand. It is 12 years since I pointed out in the L & H the fearful danger of any secret society coming under foreign domination and being used against Ireland and the Faith. I was laughed at then!'[151]

After the war, Ireland, unlike many other English-speaking countries, endured years of economic depression, which led to

---

151 Eugene to his mother, 30 May 1940, MSJA.

widespread emigration to Britain, Canada, the US and Australia. The prospect of Mount St Joseph opening a daughter house in Australia must have seemed very unlikely at the start of the 1950s. The world had shrunk after the war, however, through the development of air transport, and travel was becoming easier. Among the visitors to Rome were cardinals from across the globe coming to pay their respects to Pope Pius XII. Those of Irish descent, mainly from the US and Australia, frequently availed of the opportunity to include Ireland in their plans. One such was Cardinal Gilroy, archbishop of Sydney, who visited Roscrea on 22 December 1952 and invited the abbot to make a foundation in Sydney. At the time, Mount St Joseph was itself in debt, due to a new foundation at Nunraw, in Scotland, and to the refurbishment being carried out at Roscrea itself.[152] Acknowledging this situation, his Eminence offered to look for a suitable property in Sydney and to offer it as a gift.

Fr M. Thomas Gondal, Procurator General of the Cistercian order, was approached for permission for an Australian foundation. He approved the following:

1. the undertaking of a new foundation in Australia;
2. the acquisition of a property 'on condition that the solitude … is adequate';
3. the cost of a monk's voyage 'and that of a companion'. He recommended prudence, however, in sending a group. A loan of £10,000 could be sought.[153]

Then, quite suddenly in the autumn of 1953, a cable from Cardinal Gilroy arrived in Roscrea, stating that he had an option for some ten days on land that contained a fairly large mansion, and that he would welcome a representative from the monastery straightaway to assess its suitability. In response, 'Fr Boylan was summoned to equip himself with all that was necessary and to fly within two days. This he did!'[154] In response to Cardinal Gilroy's letter, Abbot Claffey wrote on 5 September 1953:

152 File on Australia, MSJA. In ch.4 of Ms history.
153 Claffey Papers re. Australia, 5/4, MSJA.
154 Eugene's account as related by his friend in Sydney, Fr C. J. Duffy. 'Fr Eugene Boylan in Sydney', MSJA.

I am sending one of my monks, Fr Eugene Boylan, to Australia by air. He will set out immediately the arrangements for his flight have been completed. Fr Eugene will inspect the property that is coming on the market in the Archdiocese of Sydney. He will send a report too. Fr Eugene might also be able to prepare the way for a colony of Cistercian monks by giving lectures and explaining our way of life to the Australian people.[155]

EARLY DAYS IN SYDNEY

Information about Eugene's stay in Australia is scattered, but there is an interesting and colourful account of his time there provided by a Fr C. J. Duffy of St Joseph's College, Hunter's Hill. Duffy relates that Cardinal Gilroy personally accompanied Eugene to the selected site, not far from Penrith. After an examination of the property, however, it was clear to Eugene that it was not suitable, and he so informed the Cardinal. Taken aback, Gilroy invited Eugene to take up residence at his palace at Manly, on the northern side of the city, while he (Eugene) made a thorough search in the archdiocese for a more fitting property.

A suitable site proved hard to come by. Boylan soon learned, Duffy explained, 'the geological fact that Sydney is situated in the middle of the Hawkesbury Sandstone Plateau, which carries a very light topsoil only inches deep, incapable of growing crops. The boundaries of the archdiocese are contained within this plateau except for the fertile Hawkesbury River Valley. There, however, the richness of the soil put it outside the possibility of purchase'. Eugene, meanwhile, enjoyed the opportunity of touring the whole area by car in search of the elusive property. He kept postponing the day when he would tell the Cardinal the disappointing news that he could not recommend a site in the archdiocese. Adding to Eugene's reticence was the absence of any clear reference to the amount of money available for the purchase of a future monastery.

Seeking a break from the palace, 'the active and socially

155 Claffey to Gilroy, 5 Sept. 1953, 5/4, MSJA.

inclined monk' learned that the only priest who owned a yacht on the harbour was one Fr C. J. Duffy, at the Office of Supervisor of Catholic Education for New South Wales in St Joseph's College, Hunter's Hill. Eugene, having phoned Duffy and explained who he was, received an invitation from him to stay at the college. He remained there for four weeks. Duffy wrote of him:

> He was vitally interested in all matters of politics and especially in matters ecclesiastical as well as persons ... The country and its ways appealed to his unconventional and adventurous nature, and he would have liked ... to hear that he was to be a member of the pioneer community. But underneath he had a feeling that such was not to be and so in the meantime he decided to pack in as much experiences as he could in the time available.

Duffy believed that Boylan had planned to explore the Sydney area thoroughly 'while making contacts with the suffragan bishops with a view to investigating the country dioceses. After that, he would go interstate and particularly to Victoria. And so he did.' There was no problem about invitations 'because of his personality and the glamour of his reputation, heightened by the aura of Cistercianism'. Duffy continued:

> As time went on I came to form the impression that he rated most highly as a man of charm, wit and intellect, that he was a priest through and through, and that he could divest himself of his monastic environment completely, once out of the cloister. In Australia he was on a holiday from the habit. He donned monastic garb only to say Mass, to lecture in public or to conduct religious exercises, and it was replaced at the first possible moment. He was generous with his time and accepted every invitation to give retreats and conferences as well as to grace social gatherings. As a result, he was away from the college most of the day and evening. He was in constant demand for all types of engagements.

As time passed, Gilroy revealed to Eugene that he was offering a sum of £20,000 towards a new foundation. Boylan understood that this signified no more than an initial payment.

FURTHER SEARCHES IN SYDNEY

While there is only a small amount of material in the archives covering Eugene's activities in Sydney, it is clear from what we have that there was more to Eugene's activities than reported by Duffy. The property offered by the Cardinal had been deemed unsuitable because of its inability to feed some thirty monks and because it was not sufficiently remote to ensure solitude. Eugene continued his search in the Sydney region, however, and at one point thought he had found a suitable property, named Winbourne. On 26 September 1953, he wrote to Abbot Claffey about his intention to secure the property:

> I am tackling the problem cautiously and meanwhile getting experts to report on the whole property. I shall keep looking around but feel that this is the house that the Lord has chosen … I am afraid to make a public appeal until I secure an option on a property. Masonic influence is strong and bitter.[156]

Conscious of the presence of forces hostile to Catholic developments, Eugene determined not to appeal to the public for financial assistance, but to target individuals instead. He aimed high. 'I am meeting the Prime Minister tomorrow and am going to put it to him that he must help. I can borrow the money easily, but I want to have it as a gift.' He also attended public functions with the Archbishop, which had 'many advantages'.[157]

The Winbourne project came to nothing. Already, on 25 September, Abbot Claffey had suggested, 'If necessary you may extend your search beyond the Archdiocese of Sydney', but Eugene was loath to leave Sydney. He had met a great many people who might help him in his search for a property and in the financing of it. On 3 October 1953 he informed Claffey,

156 Eugene to Claffey, 26 Sept. 1953, 5/4, MSJA.
157 Eugene to Claffey, 26 Sept. 1953, 5/4, MSJA.

I have talked with priests, doctors, farmers and various laymen and all assure me that I need have no anxiety about getting the money once we have the property. There are many other reasons for choosing Sydney. No bishop is likely to offer more than £20,000. The diocese offers great support and is the best source for vocations ... Sydney has 2,500,000 people and 25 percent are Catholic. Everybody is enthusiastic.[158]

REPUTATION AS A DRIVER

According to Duffy, Eugene 'had no car sense and was a contender for the title of the worst driver in the Commonwealth ... From the beginnings of our tours together, I realised that he was anxious to pick up as much as he could from me about driving and that he was without any experience, though he sought to convey the impression that he was knowledgeable and had even had some sort of licence. I had to be impervious to hints that I should hand over the wheel to a man without any permit to take control.'[159]

By this time, Boylan had made up his mind to buy a car in order to give himself freedom of movement during the remainder of his time in Australia. 'At length,' Duffy continued, 'he asked me to put him in touch with an adviser to help him to invest in a car, which I did. Mr Leo Benson, the one selected, fell absolutely under his charm and obtained an excellent car at a reasonable price. But before long he discovered the Achilles heel.' Benson was so concerned, after Boylan had taken control and was driving to conduct a retreat at a convent at Lewisham, 'that he phoned to know if the car had arrived in one piece. The reply was that the vehicle was in the grounds but that it had brought one of the gate posts with it ... This was the beginning of a series of phone calls to Leo from all parts of the city asking him to collect the car from the last place of an accident or collision. Fr Boylan remained

---

158 Eugene to Claffey, 3 Oct. 1953, 5/4, MSJA.
159 Until 1964 an Irish driving licence could be obtained simply by filling out a form, without any test.

unperturbed and confident, but by the time that he took off for Melbourne he left Leo in a state of mingled relief and apprehension.'

Concluding his narrative, Duffy commented, 'With the passage of time the same pattern was repeated in Victoria until we heard that the car had been wrecked after a collision with a tree on a straight highway when the driver suffered broken limbs. I never saw Fr Boylan again, and someone else must be called on for further information about the completion of the assignment and the departure of Fr Boylan from Australia.'[160]

Further information was supplied by a certain John R. Shea, 55 Burke Road, East Malvern – a suburb of Melbourne – about Eugene's time in the state of Victoria. At the request of the local curate, Fr J. Mullally, a native of Roscrea, he had loaned his car to Eugene, who was 'carless', his previous car 'having had a mishap'. Eugene had Shea's 1940 model Chevrolet for seventeen days as he travelled in search of a suitable site. Having covered some 2,000 miles, it appears that he returned the vehicle in sound condition. Shea mentioned that Fr Boylan 'had a simple meal with my late mother and myself. During the meal and afterwards he ate quite a great number of Rennies digestive tablets, explaining how different he found living outside his community.'[161]

SUCCESS IN TARRAWARRA

Despite his contacts, lectures, articles and public appearances, Eugene was unable to find a suitable site in Sydney, and he began to look elsewhere for the site of the new monastery. As indicated above, he moved to Melbourne, where he was once again in demand as a preacher and lecturer. It was unusual for a monk from an enclosed order to preach in public, and it was believed that he had received a dispensation to do so. The impact he had was described in a letter written to Fr Nivard shortly after Eugene's death: 'On the occasion of a Holy Name Rally in St Patrick's

160 Eugene's account as related by his friend in Sydney, Fr C. J. Duffy. 'Fr Eugene Boylan in Sydney', C. J. Duffy to Fr Nivard, 10/2/1966, MSJA.
161 J. R. Shea to Fr Nivard, 23-8-1964, Australia Section [Brown folder], MSJA.

Cathedral, Melbourne, he addressed an estimated one thousand men. Dressed in his white habit, he impressed the packed audience with his softly modulated, articulate and very expressive delivery.'[162]

In Melbourne, Eugene continued with his articles and public appearances, and created once again a network of supporters. Then, on 2 June 1954, after an extensive search, a property in Tarrawarra – about twenty-eight miles north-east of Melbourne – was identified and an arrangement was secured that would 'satisfy everyone'.[163] Meanwhile in Roscrea the Abbot, concerned at Eugene's seeming lack of progress in Australia, was having second thoughts. According to his own account of Eugene's life, as recorded in *Profiles in Sanctity* – a written profile of each abbot of Mount St Joseph – Claffey considered that, eight months after Eugene had left, he 'must either recall Fr Eugene or go himself to Australia'. His opinion was reinforced by another priest, Fr Stanislaus Sweeney, who said to him, 'Reverend Father, unless you go out there and see for yourself the position there will be no success'. This convinced Claffey of 'the necessity of the journey'. His determination was reinforced by his awareness that the sum allocated to purchase the monastic site was quite inadequate, and that his decision would be required to sanction the cost involved.

The date of the Abbot's departure is not clear, but it seems to have taken place before Eugene's letter of 2 June, containing the news of Tarrawarra, reached Roscrea. Taking with him his secretary, Fr Carthage O'Dea, Claffey set out for Sydney where he arrived a week later. There the two were joined by Eugene, and at once they commenced to examine possible sites in the diocese once again. 'The abbot had to inform the cardinal after a six days tour that none of them were suitable. Bidding the prelate farewell and expressing gratitude, the three Cistercians set out for Melbourne.'[164]

In Melbourne, Daniel Mannix (Archbishop of Melbourne, 1917–1963) gave them a cordial welcome and put them up in his

162 Keneth Beazley, Brisbane to Fr Nivard, 7 Sept. 1964, Grey Box, file 11, MSJA.
163 Eugene to Claffey, 2 June 1954, 5/4, MSJA.
164 Claffey,   'Profiles   in   Sanctity'.

house for several weeks. By this time, through his contacts, lectures and articles, Eugene had introduced the Cistercian way of life to much of Australia. Indeed, Abbot Claffey had earlier welcomed Eugene's articles in the *Catholic Weekly* which, he believed, 'may help to bring benefactors'.[165] Now, in Melbourne, Eugene used his contacts to finalise the acquisition of Tarrawarra. According to Dom Claffey,[166] one particular layman, a Mr Walter Broderick, was especially helpful in securing the property.

A letter from Eugene to his mother, on 19 August 1954, gives an indication of his role before and after the foundation at Tarrawarra.[167] From an address at 199 Rathdown Street, Carlton, Victoria, he wrote: 'The D. C. & Sec' – meaning Dom Camillus and his secretary – 'arrived out in Sydney, but are now in Melbourne, the guests of Dr Mannix. We have got our place but I won't tell you how much it cost. It's all borrowed in my name!!! The D.C. tells me he told you he was leaving me here. I don't think it is all as definite as that. Actually, between ourselves, there is a move on to bring me back to Caldey, and that's only one of the possibilities in the situation. Anyhow I'm here for the moment but I notice I have no job in the house. I'm a "propagandist".'

Eugene then goes on to elaborate on his role:

> I appear on the Town Hall platform with Frank Sheed and Maisie Ward next month, and I'm already down for three broadcasts. I've borrowed £70,000 and turned myself into a Private Company. I may yet finish up in jail. I've already had one car smash (not my fault!), no one hurt but £150 damage done to the car. However, the Insurance paid that. Winter is beginning to yield to spring, and the place we have got is ideal – 38 rooms and plenty of land and water. We don't get possession until 1st November. I've succeeded in finding an empty aeroplane coming out that will take fifteen of our men for £200

165 Claffey to Eugene, 14 Nov. 1953, 5/4, MSJA.
166 Claffey. Art.cit. in loc. Cit.
167 Eugene to his mother, 19 August 1954, Family Papers, MSJA.

each. T.A.A. (Trans Australian Airlines) are flying out
new planes, hence the deal. They should be coming out
in October. I don't think we should have much difficulty
in getting established here. Vocations are plentiful and
if promises are to be trusted, money should not be hard
to get. We are much in the news here, and I find myself
recognised far too frequently.

Eugene concluded with a reference that would interest his mother:
'I've heard quite a lot of good musicians. Standards are very high
here, and I was impressed at the number and excellence of the
entries at a concerto competition ...' His sisters would later mention
how much Eugene's own piano playing improved after his time in
Australia.

Before the end of 1954, the new Cistercian monastery, Notre
Dame, was in operation in Tarrawarra. The twenty men selected for
the community had arrived, and the daily High Mass and the Divine
Office were being chanted in choir by the community. Eugene had
not been appointed superior but was procurator of the foundation.[168]
'We were counting on Fr Eugene's help', according to Claffey, 'to pay
off the debt and run the farm by Australian methods.'

THE MOVE FROM AUSTRALIA

Although Eugene had had intimations of it in August 1954, it wasn't
until October that a letter came from the Abbot General to Claffey,
saying that the Belgian-founded house on the Isle of Caldey was in
serious danger of being closed down, and that the appointment of
Eugene as superior was the only hope of its survival. He also asked
Claffey to provide a novice master and one or two more priests. 'In
due course,' Claffey wrote, 'we complied with his wishes.'[169]

A small island of about three square miles, Caldey is situated
in the Bristol Channel about two-and-a-half miles from the town
of Tenby in South Wales. At the end of 1950, Eugene had given a
retreat there to the community, which he described to a friend at the

---

168 Typed Ms. Biography of Eugene Boylan, p. 32, MSJA.
169 Claffey, 'Profiles in Sanctity', MSJA.

time as a 'very mixed community, with several French, two Irish, and all English novices, except a Pole and a Norwegian. But they gave me the doubtful compliment of believing that my French was better than their English, which made direction difficult'.[170] The 'French', in fact, were mostly French-speaking Belgians. His retreat had made a good impression on the monks, and he was remembered when the question of a new superior arose in 1954.

Although he learned of his appointment in October that year, Eugene did not leave Australia until the following January. He had, no doubt, matters to tidy up and information to pass on to his successor as procurator. Besides, he had committed himself to reading a paper at the first Australian Liturgical Congress in Melbourne in January. Following that engagement, on 6 January, he and Abbot Claffey flew back to England and thence to Ireland. After a short stay, Eugene made his way to Caldey, where he arrived on 2 February 1955.[171]

170 Typed document on Eugene and Caldey, MSJ 5/5/5 no.1, MSJA. See also Eugene to Colonel Cave, 8 January 1951, MSJA.
171 Claffey, 'Profiles in Sanctity', p. 32, MSJA.

CHAPTER 8

CALDEY ISLAND, 1955–59

Dom Eugene preaching on Caldey Island.

Eugene had spent some eighteen months in Australia, where he had succeeded in his mission to find and purchase a suitable property for a new foundation. In what had been largely a one-man venture, he had shown a gift for public relations and fundraising. He had hoped to stay on, but many of his Cistercian colleagues wondered how he would fit in as a member of a team, rather than as its head. It was soon recognised, however, that the gifts he had demonstrated in Australia might be the saving of the Cistercian foundation at Caldey. Eugene probably left Australia with a mixture of elation and sorrow, but Caldey offered him a command of his own and another stiff challenge. His appointment was generally recognised as a last effort to set the monastery in Caldey on its feet financially and, in view of the fact that future novices were likely to come from Britain and Ireland,[172] to establish it as an English-speaking community.

Monasticism on Caldey Island

The history of the monastery in Caldey is an unusual one. It is the site of a monastic settlement dating from early Christian times. With the revival of monastic life in the Anglican Church at the beginning of the twentieth century, it was acquired by a group of Anglican Benedictines, who eventually were received, as a community, into the Roman Catholic Church. Finding their situation economically critical, they left the island in 1928 and settled at Prinknash in Gloucester. Shortly afterwards, the Holy See requested the Abbot General of the Cistercians to consider buying the island in order to maintain the monastic tradition there. In response, the Belgian Abbey of Scourmont, in the Chimay district, offered to open a new foundation there. This meant that the Caldey community was mostly Belgian, and when the Second World War began ten years later, almost the entire body of monks was called to the Belgian and French colours, leaving only a skeleton group to keep the monastery going during the war. Many of those who returned to Caldey when peace was established in 1945 came back with weakened health. Finding their house in a financially precarious condition, they did not have the energy or skill to set it on a sound footing once more.

The post-war years brought an influx of English novices, and an Irish novice master, Fr Albert, who was an experienced spiritual director, was sent from Roscrea. The ethos remained continental, however, with the mother house at Chimay providing a large annual

172 Typed document on Eugene and Caldey, MSJA.

subsidy. The Belgian monks determined the style of life in the community, creating difficulties for the younger men.

In addition, living on an island, however excellent the situation for solitude and contemplation, added to the community's financial problems. 'Difficulties of transport and of marketing produce, with added costs, regular periods during winter of being cut off from the mainland, and the general uncertainty of communication in winter, render the island situation extremely difficult.'[173]

By the early 1950s the monastery was struggling to remain viable. While there was a promising number of novices, survival still depended on the subsidy from Belgium. The house in Caldey was technically a Coventual Priory, and was led by a prior – 'though the prior was Abbot in all but name'. By 1954 the situation had become too much for then prior, Dom Albert, whose health had been impaired by internment, and he resigned on medical advice. An official Visitation was carried out and it was put to the community that there was little point in having a routine election for a new prior until the future of the community could be more clearly secured.

In these circumstances, it was agreed that a new superior should be appointed for a period of five years, and that the new prior (as he would be called) must be either Irish or English.

Remembering the retreat given by Eugene in 1950, many of the monks put his name forward for the role, as noted above. This suggestion was taken up by higher authorities and communicated to Dom Claffey just as Eugene was preparing to return from Australia.

CHALLENGES AND TRIALS AT CALDEY

Dom Eugene, as he would be henceforth known, had three main tasks at Caldey. First of all, he had to take the very disparate elements in the monastery and mould them into a harmonious community, without suppressing the enrichment each one had to offer. Secondly, he had to make Caldey into an English-speaking monastery, since its future lay in recruitment from Britain and not in dependence on foreign support. Finally, he had to make the monastery financially

173 Typed document on Eugene and Caldey, MSJA.

independent.[174]

On 27 March 1955, two months after arriving in Caldey, Eugene informed Abbot Claffey that there was in the monastery an 'air of defeatism that is hard to overcome'. He added, however, that the discipline within the community was improving and that 'for attendance in choir and obedience, the community are most edifying'.[175] Issues of discipline were to remain, however. In his talks to the community, Eugene sought to deepen their religious spirit, to promote the love and service of God and neighbour that enriched community life, and to encourage prayer for vocations. He was hopeful about vocations, as there were 'applications … coming in and if we can weather the next few years we should be able to pull through'.[176] He saw the future lying with the younger men, and he determined that the 'juniors should be sent to Rome for higher studies'.[177] Among those he sent was Eugene's successor in Caldey, James Wicksteed – known in religion as Samson Wicksteed – and John Gran, a young Norwegian who would become Bishop of Oslo.

In an interview about his memories of Caldey, Dom Samson Wicksteed admitted frankly that when Eugene arrived the community 'was really anarchic'. Quite a number of the monks – senior members who were mostly Belgians – had failed to settle down after the war. With his first task in mind, Eugene was very conciliatory at the beginning, but he was also forthright. Gradually his attitude hardened, however, especially towards obstinate opponents. 'He could take a lot, but there was a flash point beyond which you could not go … He could give a frightful dressing down.'[178]

A notable example of this was the case of Br Thomas, who had effectively run the place. When Eugene appointed a new cellarer, Br Thomas objected strongly. Having received a strong rebuke from Eugene, he bolted, but came back after a few days. He was 'a very difficult man to handle', Samson explained.[179] When asked if Eugene

174 Typed document on Eugene and Caldey, MSJA..

175 Eugene to Claffey, 27 March 1955, Claffey Papers, MSJA.

176 Eugene to Claffey, 27 March 1955, MSJA.

177 Claffey, 'Profiles in Sanctity', p. 32, MSJA.

178 Fr Nivard's interview with Dom Sarson (*sic*), Abbot of Caldey, MSJA.

179 Fr Nivard's interview with Abbot Samson, MSJA.

seemed a holy man during his time at Caldey, Samson replied, 'Certainly. But he was very human. He could be very generous, but he could be petty at times'.[180]

Eugene's second task, transforming the house into an English-speaking community, was a problem where the older members were concerned. The Divine Office remained in Latin, of course, but Eugene's sermons and talks to the community were in English. The most that could be said about Eugene's record in this regard was suggested by a community member later interviewed in Caldey by Fr Nivard. Asked about Eugene's impact on the Caldey community, he remarked that 'it was a much less *foreign* community when he left'.

The same person considered Eugene a spiritual man who 'did great good here', but who could be obstinate and was rather offensive to the Belgians. He also mentioned that he 'was a great fidget – he could never sit still', adding that 'it was difficult to reconcile that with the impression of placidity that you get from his books on prayer'. He also said that he had a temper, but acknowledged that Eugene '*had* to assert his authority here'.[181]

To achieve complete success in the first two tasks he faced in Caldey was virtually impossible. The third task – the achievement of financial independence – might seem more straightforward, but it was complicated by the fact that it was intertwined with the other two tasks. Quite soon after his arrival at Caldey, Eugene reported to Abbot Claffey in Roscrea:

> Things are not quite as bad as I expected. Everybody is very friendly and Father Albert is a very great help. There is no Second Superior … There seems to be some hope of developing a sale of herbs and lavender … However, only time will tell how the economic side will do … I am going as slowly and gently as I can.[182]

The absence of a second superior left all authority in Eugene's hands, and this made any absence of his from the house very noticeable.

180 Fr Nivard's interview with Abbot Samson, MSJA.
181 Fr Nivard's interview with a Caldey priest, whose name is difficult to decipher, MSJA.
182 Eugene to Claffey, 3 Feb. 1955, Claffey Papers, MSJ 5/4, MSJA.

His later problems with the Belgian members might have been eased had he appointed a Belgian as a second superior. In fact, he considered this, but never made the appointment.[183]

DEVELOPING THE PERFUMERY

There was some form of perfumery in operation in the monastery on Eugene's arrival, and a small shop had been set up on the mainland in Tenby. During the summer, when tourists came to the island in large numbers, Eugene realised that if the monks could sell more to these visitors it would help to stabilise the community's finances. On 17 February 1955 he wrote to Abbot Claffey about the financial situation, mentioning some of the difficulties and possible solutions. He also referred to the Belgian mother house, which continued to pay a subsidy towards the Caldey foundation.

> The immediate problem is to reduce the annual deficit which Scourmount has to pay every year (£3,000–£4,000). The 'continental' section of the community are quite willing to go on letting Scourmount pay, and are quite opposed to any expansion of the shop, which I intend to develop. We can increase our income from £1,000–£2,000, by lavender and herbs. The 'Hall' has been turned into a poultry farm for intensive production of chickens, and this should help also.[184]

One of the monks, a former chemist in Poland, developed a new perfume, using the fragrance of lavender plants.[185] Seeing this as offering opportunities for increased income, Eugene set about seeking advice and contacts. Encouraged by the responses, and in order to publish the distinctive Caldey perfume, he got in touch with the best known fashion designer in Dublin, Sybil Connolly, who had access to an American market. Eventually, through this contact, and through other contacts he had from his books and articles, he

183 Fr Nivard's interview with Abbot Samson, MSJA.
184 Eugene to Claffey, 17 Feb. 1955, MSJA. Scourmount was the wealthy Belgian mother house which was supporting the Caldey foundation financially.
185 Virginia Scott, article in *The Progress* (American Catholic magazine), 4 March 1960, MSJ 5/5/7 no. 5, MSJA. External Documents.

gained publicity for the perfume, which became popular in Britain and gained outlets in Australia. Eugene was said to 'have made contacts in New York to introduce the perfume on Fifth Avenue – at $37.50 an ounce'.[186] The seeming incongruity of a contemplative monk being involved in the marketing of perfume caught the attention of newspapers, as Eugene intended; it also caused unease among some old school friends as well as among some clergy.

His friend from his schooldays, Donal Flood, remembered meeting Eugene

> when he was on the perfume business ... perhaps at the Unicorn (restaurant). I remember saying to him "that's a queer thing you've gone into" ... It wasn't the last thing I'd have thought of Kevin Boylan (doing) ... Lord No! But it was the last thing I'd have thought of Cistercians doing ... People have to live even if they are religious, but he went into it all in a characteristic way ... I mean in a most unreligious and worldly way ... He went off and commercialised the thing, got the proper sort of bottle and so on ... I've never seen the stuff but he told me all about it ... Any time I met him in Dublin he was dining alone ... always alone, always on his own, the lone bird.'[187]

It never seems to have occurred to the censorious Donal that a quiet meal might have been a welcome oasis for Eugene in a busy day, or that he was not accustomed to speaking at meals.

EXPANDING THE BUSINESS

Meanwhile in Caldey, in June 1955, Eugene was able to report hopeful progress, while also highlighting a major difficulty in expanding the business:

> The shop we opened in Tenby is doing very well and from what I have seen of the summer season, I have no doubt that the economy problem can be solved, by poultry, market gardening and perfume. It will take time, as the

186 Scott, *The Progress*, MSJA.
187 Flood interviewed by Fr Nivard, MSJA,

great difficulty is all the more acute at the moment, since of our 36 men, 30 are bound to choir; of these, 18 have to do either their studies or their novitiate. But please God time will soften that problem. The future really depends on our getting lay-brothers.[188]

On 16 January 1956, Eugene wrote from Caldey to his mother to congratulate her on her seventy-eighth birthday. Writing in the cavalier style that she seemed to cherish, he regretted he was not there to celebrate with her. Then, after making reference to letters and friends, this notoriously poor driver told of a nightmare car journey of 200 miles he had made in Wales. 'The drive back was drastic. The first fifty miles on sheets of ice and all the way along ice patches. They talk about our Irish roads. You should see the roads through the Welsh mountains!' Then, in the same letter and with remarkable insensitivity, Eugene mentioned that a friend of his, Mrs Cave, aged seventy-eight years, had come to visit him in Caldey. One of her several sisters lived in Dún Laoghaire, and he had suggested to her that she might stay in his mother's spare bedroom while visiting this sister, or that she might perhaps make arrangements to stay there permanently. One wonders what his elderly mother felt about such gratuitous suggestions!

Speaking of Caldey, Eugene told his mother that 'things go on as usual. I've just taken the law into my own hands and ordered the planting of 10 acres of cabbages and signed a contract for extensive drainage. If it's a flop, I'll never be let forget!' He finished with a flourish. 'Sorry I'm not there to crack a bottle! – but take the will for the deed and do it yourself. I'll say Mass for you in the morning.'[189]

By April 1956, Eugene appeared to accept that, while the attitude of older members of the community would not, or could not, be changed, the community, nevertheless, had a future. 'The house is settling down slowly. Things are by no means yet what they should be, but there is a definite improvement and I am not without great hope for the future. But there is no good in trying to force old

188 Eugene to Claffey, 26 June 1955, MSJ 5/4, MSJA.
189 Eugene to his mother, 16 Jan, 1956, MSJA.

113

men to change their ways, so that I have to rely on the young men.

In 1957 British television carried a programme about the monastery on Caldey Island which elicited some interest. The press reports suggested that Dom Eugene would have made a very successful 'public relations officer'[190] – ironically a role in marked contrast to the monastic life itself and to Eugene's teaching as prior.

THE SPIRITUAL TEACHING OF PRIOR EUGENE

In the course of his sermons and talks, Eugene appealed to the idealism of his younger monks while seeking to deepen the spirituality of all the community. From September 1957 to May 1959, a novice at the time, known as Br Christopher, was so impressed that he rushed into the noviciate after each talk and wrote down what he had heard. He subsequently typed these talks and had them printed.[191] Although they are filtered through the memory and interpretation of just one member of the congregation, they provide some indication of the thought of Prior Boylan and the themes he frequently addressed. As Br Christopher himself observed, they appear to be 'the only records of this charismatic monk's teachings to his own Cistercian Order'.

In different ways, Eugene often emphasised the qualities necessary in a monk's life. In his talks and sermons he was clearly very conscious of the mixed nature of his audience – some men highly educated, others with very limited education. On 6 August 1958, his theme was 'Obedience'. The tendency to independence is deep within us, he told the monks.

> We resent deep down being 100% dependent on God ...
> This independence causes a resentment against religious
> obedience ... If we are spiritually poor and realise our
> utter dependence on God for absolutely everything – we
> shall love obedience, because by it we know we are doing
> the Father's will. If we do the Father's will – we do it in
> union with Jesus. And we do the most important thing in

190 Kathleen Hartland (a cousin) to Eugene, 24 June 1957, Grey Box, File 15, MSJA.
191 Br Christopher. 'A Record of Sermons and Talks by Dom Eugene Boylan O.C.S.O at
    Caldey Island Priory, 1957–1959', 5/5/4, no. 3, MSJA. (Black Box with green back.)

the world, we bear forth Jesus again.

Two days later, on a somewhat similar theme, Eugene spoke of 'Dependence on God'.

> God created us free beings – free to cooperate with him or free to be independent … Choir monks are especially called in their private and communal life and prayer to recognise their real poverty and the greatness of God and to realise how dependent they are on God. The higher we advance in the spiritual life, the more dependent we are on God. We come to realise we can do nothing alone.

The following day, 9 August 1958, the emphasis was on 'Confidence in God'. He came back to speak of spiritual poverty and underlined God's mercy.

> If we place our confidence in our own virtue, strength, fervour etc., then our confidence is only as strong as we are, it is limited. When the day of temptation comes we shall be weak and fail because our confidence fails … On the other hand confidence in God through spiritual poverty is unlimited, and will not fail. There is nothing we cannot hope for, however bad we are, or in whatever bad and unsuitable circumstances we find ourselves. God delights in showing his mercy by turning impossible things into good.

Eugene took 'Obedience and Charity' as his theme on a number of occasions. On 22 September 1958, he noted how the great precepts of the Old Law were confirmed by Christ: Thou shalt love the Lord thy God with thy whole heart, mind, strength and soul; and Thou shalt love thy neighbour as thyself.

> This is also the main object of religious life put to us by obedience and fraternal charity. We love God by doing his will that is revealed to us by religious obedience, which involves everything down to the smallest detail. We love each other by fraternal charity even down to the smallest and most annoying details … If we keep these precepts, we fulfil our obligations … and give Christ new

life on earth ... Christ said what you do to the least of
these little ones you do unto me. Therefore, all that we do
to individuals or to the community is taken by Christ as
done to himself. Charity applies even more to the praying
for each other's supernatural needs.

Later, on an unspecified date, Eugene returned again to this theme,
but in a more pointed manner, in a talk on 'Judging':[192]

We do not know what each other is suffering, nor of the
graces or lack of graces they have, nor do we know their
vocation ... We are all burdens to the community, and
we have to carry one another's burdens. We came as men
and we find men – not angels – in the community, and
we find men as superiors. It is God's glory in his plan
for us to make saints out of imperfect material and with
imperfect instruments. We all have a part to play in the
sanctification of others and others have an essential part
to play in the sanctification of us ... We are deficient
agents when we do our best (which is rare). Only Christ
can fulfil our obligations by our union with him and by
the daily Mass.'

Eugene then reiterated that 'Christ is in each of our brothers and
takes the very smallest thing done for or against them as done for
or against him'. He then continued in a way that must have focused
attention:

Allowances must be made for the young brethren who
are brash, energetic, critical and always judging, but
who are soon sorted out by monastic life itself. Far more
important and trying, great allowances must be made for
the old and infirm. Many have had different education
to us in their novitiate, some have had an inadequate
novitiate due to more lax conditions by a foundation.
Many are incapacitated in body or mind through many
years of excessive suffering and toil. In any case – all
vocations to the monastery are due to the trials, sufferings

192 Br Christopher, 'A Record of Sermons', pp. 23–4, MSJA.

and fidelities of the older brethren. They deserve respect as spiritual parents. We must respect each other always especially those of other nationalities.

On the Second Sunday of Lent, 22 February 1959, the Prior sought to strengthen his brethren by a sermon on 'Faith', much of which seems to be autobiographical. Eugene spoke of the apostles' difficulty with faith at the Transfiguration, and again at the Passion. He then continued:

How much more difficult for us who are separated by so many years and miles from the temporal existence of Christ ... After we have entered a monastery and start to advance, to ourselves we seem to lose everything and get worse and worse. Fervour goes, prayer is vague and dissatisfying, we seem to be getting nowhere – in fact we have to keep going by sheer will in faith alone. We have to believe in eternity, we have to believe in the use of our lives, that God is going to sanctify us through our incompetent superiors. We have to believe that we will rise after death and that God is working for us in his infinite mercy in the smallest and greatest circumstances in our lives. Eventually, we have to live by faith alone ... We give up very real things for things which can only be believed in. This is impossible for us to do alone. It requires much prayer and union with Christ ... We should always ask for an increase of faith in the sacraments. All that destroys our faith or is an obstacle will certainly halt us on the way to perfection. We must be careful always to believe in God's action in our superiors and all they do. If we start judging them we are heading for trouble ... We learn in religion how God can give grace through incompetent superiors. It is the same for Providence. Once we stop believing and start judging, we fail.

It should be noted that Eugene's teaching on obedience to incompetent superiors and its acceptance as part of God's will was very much a feature of religious life before the Second Vatican

Council. It was considerably modified as a result of the council.

In his addresses, as in his writings, Christ was always central for Eugene. On 2 March 1959, he focused on the 'Humanity of Christ'. It sometimes happens, he said, that those following a more intellectual life in theology

> dispense themselves with the Sacred Humanity of Christ. They have misread about carnal sensible love and spiritual love and in order to advance they drop the first to concentrate on the second ... This action is extremely dangerous ... We must never dispense with the Humanity of Christ, nor leave his Passion and life without periodically returning to it. It is fatal to try and be angels when we are men. We must love God with our whole being, body and soul – sensible and spiritual. There is nothing impure or degrading about the so-called carnal love ... We must always have the Sacred Humanity with us in some form – either a more human 'Jesus' – or a more spiritual Christ (God and man, mystical body etc). It changes as we do.

As a final extract from Br Christopher's compilation, Eugene's talk on 'The Holy Spirit and the Monk's Vocation' seems appropriate. It was given on 11 May 1959, at a time when, as he notes, the signs of spring were evident. He told the gathered community:

> Our life is a sacrifice of ourselves. We cannot do this, we are not strong enough, we need the Holy Spirit. This sacrifice is our sanctification. We need the Holy Spirit to submit to the will of God – no matter what it costs. We cannot hope to do this alone. The holy will of God is working for our decrease and Christ's increase. Hence we lose more and more and become less self-centred and more Christ centred – impossible without the Holy Spirit. Our life is a long pruning – like pear trees which must be pruned if they are to bear fruit; or the beautiful apple blossom which we can now see but which must die away if there is to be any fruit. So our talents etc. are only

our blossom – these have to die and go if we are to bear fruit. Our vocation is one of tremendous dignity – that of being another Christ. For this Christ sends us his own Spirit – the Holy Spirit to help us.

Br Christopher's compilation ends shortly after this. He himself left the monastery after twenty months for reasons of health. Having returned to his former life as R. Christopher K. Alcock, he rejoined the RAF for sixteen years, and then continued flying commercially for forty-seven years, until 1999. He married in 1962 and had twelve children. As a layman, he visited Caldey on a regular basis, and Dom Eugene's teaching remained, as he expressed it, 'an inspiration to my way of life and prayer'.[193]

THE ELECTION OF AN ABBOT

In 1958, Notre Dame in Tarrawarra was raised to the status of an abbey. The following year, with an improved financial situation and better relations within the community, Eugene petitioned that Caldey too be raised to the status of an abbey. This was granted, and the election of an abbot by the community duly took place. Given all he had done for the survival of Caldey, Eugene expected to be elected abbot, but it was not to be. Why he was not chosen is not clear. That there was some dissatisfaction with him is suggested by one extant comment from a member of the community, a Fr Dominic, who does not, it should be noted, come across as an impartial commentator.

Fr Dominic commented that Fr Boylan's retreat in 1958 was the best he had attended, but added that there was a big difference between his monastic life and what he preached. 'I did not think much of his monastic life. He took too much liberty. He did not understand the diversity of the community here … He never came to chapter when someone other than himself was preaching … He did not like our diet. His rough way of complaining in chapter put me off.'[194] The man chosen as abbot was young and English, which suggests that

193 Br. Christopher, 'A Record of Sermons', footnote on p. 83, MSJA.
194 Fr Dominic, Caldey, 'Interviews' conducted by Fr Nivard, MSJA.

the votes of the younger members may have been decisive.

Eugene was disappointed, and seems to have expressed his feelings to Dom Claffey. Three days later, the latter's reply offered Eugene consolation and encouragement. 'Your letter of 2 October came today. I can quite understand your feelings of the moment but I know also that you will have accepted the result as God's will in your regard. He has other designs for you. You have "saved Caldey" and that is what you were called home from Australia to do.'[195] Eugene did indeed accept the decision as God's will, and saw reasons why he should be happy that he was not elected. Writing once again to Dom Claffey, on Sunday 4 October 1959, he observed that 'the position of "Superior Toleratus" is not an easy one and I have a great sense of relief in being freed from it'.[196]

On that same day, in a letter to his mother, he explained how the result had been determined. It had only been officially announced that morning, because on the previous Thursday a postulation had had to be sent to Rome concerning 'the election of a man, who was not senior enough'. The requested dispensation had come through the night before, he wrote, and 'Dom Samson Wicksteed was installed this morning'. The new Abbot was going to Belgium for his retreat, Eugene continued, and he had asked Eugene to carry on until his return. It would be more than a week, therefore, before he arrived in Dublin. 'I had told the Abbot General when in France', Eugene declared, 'what was going to happen, and gave him the name of the next abbot. He did not believe me.' Eugene then went on:

> You cannot pull a house like this together and retain votes, *before* election. They have picked the right man and he will be in a much stronger position than I was or ever would have been. I don't know what the Roscrea man's plans for me are but there is a fearfully difficult situation there and which I shall have much difficulty in avoiding being drawn into it! (*sic*). Australia is not much better. Raising funds there would – for me – be quite an unpleasant job.

195 Claffey to Eugene, 5 Oct. 1959, 5/5/1 no. 15, MSJA.
196 Eugene to Claffey, 4 Oct. 1959, 5/4, MSJA.

However, I expect the Lord has something up his sleeve. He then told his mother that it would be a while before he got to Roscrea because he would be giving a retreat 'in our own monastery at Portglenone, County Antrim, on 23 October'.[197]

APPRECIATION AND GRATITUDE

Eugene received many messages expressing disappointment and surprise at his not being elected abbot. The local bishop wrote from Wrexham House on 8 October, stating that he was more sorry than he could say that Eugene was leaving Caldey. 'My hope had been to have blessed you as its first abbot. This is not in any way an implied condemnation of the community's choice but an expression of my own personal wishes'.[198] Br Benignus, writing from Mellifont Abbey, Collon, Co. Louth, was sorry 'for Caldey's sake' that he was not elected, and he hoped that Dom Samson would follow in Eugene's footsteps and not allow Caldey to fall back to the state it was in when Eugene took over.[199] 'It was thought for a long time that it could not be made self-supporting,' he wrote. 'You have shown how it could. I do hope they will get enough English and Irish postulants to make it an English-speaking Community.'[200]

Eugene had got on very well with local people on Caldey and in Tenby. 'Many volunteers, men and women, had spent summers during his time at Caldey working for the monastery, staffing the souvenir shops and serving in the guest house and tea rooms ... They were loyal to Dom Eugene and even when they criticised him, they did so with affection and admiration.'[201] They readily expressed their sadness at his departure. There is an extant account of comments by the villagers of Caldey about Eugene , compiled by one of his admirers, a Miss Jill John. It contains their recollections of the prior, as well as their

197 Eugene to his mother, 4 Oct. 1959, 5/5/1 no. 15, MSJA.
198 Bishop, Wrexam House, Wales to Eugene, 8 Oct. 1959, 5/4, MSJA.
199 Fr Nivard's interview with Dom Wicksteed, who succeeded Eugene, indicates that the Perfume trade continued to bring in £1,000 a year for five years more, but was then squeezed out by bigger competitors.
200 Br Benignus (was actually the abbot), Mellifont Abbey, Co. Louth to Eugene, 7 Oct. 1959, 5/5/1 no. 12, MSJA.
201 Kinsella, *Dom Eugene Boylan*, p. 16.

impressions – and no doubt prejudices – about the monks as well.
    Prior Eugene was too straight. He never got credit for it.
    The English could not stand him. Fr Nivard won't learn
    any good about Prior Boylan up there because they won't
    admit it. We loved Fr Eugene – He was one of ourselves.
    He liked the poor, and he'd just breeze into the house and
    have a cup of tea. He used often come to watch rugby
    matches on TV ... and in the spring to watch boxing ...
    He was completely at home and you'd never think he was
    anyone. You'd never think he was brilliant. He was just
    one of ourselves. We loved him.[202]

On 13 October, a former resident of Caldey, Audrey Muffett,
wrote to Eugene. Her husband had been a police officer on Caldey
before they moved to Haverfordwell. Addressing him as 'Father
Eugene' she expressed her sorrow that he was leaving Caldey. 'I shall
remember our brief meetings with pleasure. You have always shown
such kindness and goodness to me and my family. Thank You.' She
then went on to speak of her children in a way that suggests that
Eugene knew them. It is also evident from Mrs Muffett's letter that
he had spoken to her about his mother, as he seems to have done
with friends. She observed, 'You will be glad I expect to be returning
home. You will be happy to see a little more of your family. I hope
your amazing mother is well. She will be glad to see you back.' The
letter finished with a prayer. This friendship with the locals, as well
as his absences on business, was perhaps what Father Dominic
had in mind when he criticised Eugene because 'he took too much
liberty' in his monastic life.

    An appropriate footnote to Eugene's time in Caldey was an
invitation he received, a few years later, to the episcopal consecration
of Fr John Gran, a former member of the community in Caldey who
had been appointed bishop of Oslo. Eugene realised that he would
probably be asked to speak on the occasion, and he determined to
do so in Norwegian. With considerable difficulty, he managed to
obtain a tape of the language and used a tape recorder to help his

202 'Interviews'. Miss Jill John's account of the Villagers of Caldey, MSJA.

pronunciation. With his facility in languages, he acquired a certain competence within a relatively short time. A Benedictine friend, Father Wulstan Phillipson of Downside Abbey also attended the consecration. He reported, 'At the dinner in the evening, Abbot Boylan brought the house down by speaking for about five minutes in Norwegian, specially learnt for the occasion, and went on to say that if they found their new bishop difficult they must make allowances for the fact that he had been several years under an Irish superior at Caldey!' Wulstan's abiding memory of Eugene was 'his shining humility and glorious sense of humour'.[203]

The final word on Eugene's time in Caldey may be left to Dom Columban Mulcahy, who knew him very well: 'In Caldey, one said afterwards, that he had preached many striking sermons, but none so striking as the graceful way he stepped down when Dom Samson was elected. It took a big man to do it.'[204]

203 Fr Wulstan Phillipson to Fr Nivard, 31 Oct. 1968, Grey Folder I, 14–17, MSJA.
204 Dom Columban interviewed by Fr Nivard, 1964, MSJA.

CHAPTER 9

WRITER, CORRESPONDENT AND RETREAT DIRECTOR

From the 1940s to the start of the 1960s, despite the range of duties that occupied his time and attention, Eugene devoted much of his time to writing for publication. While obedience, as we have seen, was for him an essential requirement in a monk's life, it comes as a surprise, nevertheless, to find him quoted as saying, 'Anything I have written since I became a monk was because I was asked to write it, and the request was framed in a mood that was categorically imperative'.[205] There seems to be no further evidence of an 'imperative' of this kind. The statement refers, one presumes, to his published writings, as distinct from his correspondence. Even with respect to his published work, however, it seems likely that any request for him to write was framed in general terms – 'You should write about spiritual matters' – rather than as a 'categorical imperative'. He kept his abbot informed about his writing and, of course, required permission to have his books published.

He was self-conscious about his literary style, as he revealed in his strong assertion, 'As regards belles-lettres, I am an absolute Philistine'. At school, he had only read the English classics when and insofar as he had to. 'The only writer whose style meant anything to me apart from its content was Chesterton,' he asserted. 'I have never had any patience with the writer, or the reader, who is more concerned with how one says things that with what one says.' He then went on to give a description of a good style, seemingly unaware of what he was doing. 'If one has something to say that is worth saying, why not say it directly, with clarity and conciseness, rather than drawing it out at length and wrapping it up in a wealth of verbiage that only obscures its meaning.'

On the effect of his writing, he claimed that 'any good that has been done through my pen is due to the sanctity of the community

205 Hoehn, *Catholic Authors.*

in which I live and to the Divine Office which we daily sing in public'.[206] His reverence for some of the older monks in Roscrea and for their sanctity is well established, and it was noted that he not only enjoyed singing the Divine Office with his fine singing voice, but that he had mastered the Latin texts, had imbibed the spirituality of the Divine Office, and really prayed it.

CONCERN FOR THE CHURCH AND FORMATION

Eugene's extant letters to his family, friends and those who sought his advice manifest different aspects of his personality and interests. On 15 December 1949, he wrote to his friend Peter Flood OSB, to congratulate him on his profession. He was delighted that he had been sent to Rome: 'It's not so much a question of theology as of everything else'. Eugene then expressed his views and talked about his own life. He had heard that important people in Rome were 'insisting that the *woman* in *Genesis* III, 15, has no reference *whatever* to Our Lady ... not even a typical one. This rather upsets my apple cart.' About his life he added, 'At the moment I'm teaching Dogma [and Philosophy as a *locum tenens* (substitute)] and being Master of Scholastics (18 of them) and generally trying to reconcile the lay sinners with their Saviour, so that my time is pretty well taken up.'[207]

The following day, Eugene wrote in response to a letter from Flood, saying that in regard to studies for the priesthood, he agreed with Flood about the limitations of Rome. He thought there might be 'room for a new centre in England with more freedom of action than Dominican or S.J. traditions allow of'. He felt that Ireland was 'hopelessly hidebound with conventional inertia'. Having been impressed by a visit to Ealing Abbey, he said he had marked it out 'as *the* place to send clerical vocations'. Then, on a different line of thought, Eugene suggested that the best hope of England's conversion lay with the Benedictines. 'Holiness was the first essential,' he affirmed. He then went on to say that 'quite a number

206 Hoehn, *Catholic Authors*.
207 Eugene to Peter Flood, 15 Dec. 1949, 5/5/1 no. 12, MSJA.

of Mayfair "mystics" come as far as Roscrea looking for direction since the death of Father Stuart in Farm Street. A Colonel Cave was with me recently. He commanded his lot in Burma during the war. At 50, he has offered to become a priest for work in the Sudan', and he had been accepted. 'I sent him to Fr Martindale SJ, who handled him very badly, but he managed to fix him up.'

Finally, in that same letter, Eugene expressed displeasure with the excessive control and conservatism of the Irish Church. 'I fired my first shot in the attack on the clerical problem in Ireland by publishing in book form some articles I wrote for the USA. The American target allowed me say things that would have been resented if addressed to the Irish. *The Irish Ecclesiastical Record* published some very critical comments on the relation between the clergy and laity in France. I hear the editor has been rapped on the knuckles for letting such comments appear. Every word therein applied to Ireland!'[208]

The following year, on 25 October 1950, Eugene wrote once more to Flood, speaking once again, and at greater length, about his concern for Colonel Cave. Cave was in Rome, Eugene wrote, and would benefit from meeting Flood. 'There is a friend of mine,' he began, 'a rather interesting character, at the Beda (College). He was in command in the Southern Sudan when the war broke out. He then wangled a command in (General) Wyngates group in Burma, and he is actually the man who kept the Burma Road going. At 52 he has been accepted as a student for the secular priesthood in S. Sudan and started off at the Beda in October. He would like to meet you ... You will find him a most interesting character. His father was a famous meteorologist, and he is connected with the Kerrs of Scotland. He has climbed the Himalayas etc. ... quite a person but rather at sea as a student in Rome.'[209]

It is clear in a later letter, written on 8 January 1951, that Flood and Cave had indeed met. This gave rise to some observations by Eugene about the state of formation in the Church. 'I can't quite

208 Eugene to Peter Flood, 16 Dec. 1949, MSJA.
209 Eugene to Peter Flood, 25 Oct. 1950, MSJA.

understand the system which seems common to most religious and clerical establishments in Rome ... of sending men there to study and then arranging things so that they have completely insufficient time to do so. Our own men are in an almost (similar) position, and Cave says that this is his biggest problem in the Beda.' Eugene then mentioned that Cave's aunt 'is one of the Kerrs ... (She) comes over here every year ... and gives me the inside history of the Church in London.' In recounting his conversations with her, Eugene partly repeated himself: 'Ever since Fr Stuart died a number of people in Mayfair are like sheep without a shepherd. There's great scope there for a competent director, who is not hidebound by the customs of his own order or the conventions of a time that is as dead as the dodo.' Eugene added that his prayers were always with Flood, and he asked for his prayers in return. 'It's very easy to drift on to a mud bank in my life and there are none of the fortuitous contacts that inspire one to the efforts necessary to get going again.'[210]

Eugene's mention of a free-spirited 'competent director' calls to mind a comment Abbot Columban Mulcahy made about him. Mulcahy claimed that as a moralist Eugene adhered to traditional theology but that he was not conservative. He gave as an example Eugene's attitude to the commonly held idea that there was no 'parvity of matter' (i.e. trivial matter) in relation to the sixth commandment. Eugene would not accept that notion, Mulcahy wrote, and wanted the relevant section on moral teaching to be entirely revised.[211]

Further indications of Eugene's unhappiness with customary practice and thinking was expressed in a letter to his sister at Glencairn Abbey, written on 3 October 1961. He explained that the need to replace a French teacher at the Abbey school meant that his attempt 'to tackle the book on the religious life which I would like to have finished before the (Vatican) Council' was being delayed. 'I've been planning some high pressure attacks on the Holy See, urging a restatement of the principles and the purpose of religious life. The real things are being squeezed out under the pressure of

210 Eugene to Peter Flood, 8 Jan. 1951, MSJA.
211 Dom Columban interviewed by Fr Nivard, 1964, MSJA.

"work". Even in our order, the number of religious, male and female, who can't (or at least don't) get sufficient time for spiritual reading etc. is alarmingly large.' This problem, he continued, was closely connected 'with two of the problems which seem to plague most of our convents – financial shortage and bad health.'[212]

That same year, in a letter to Mulcahy, Eugene looked forward to the Council making 'better provision for the spiritual direction of women (nuns). Even if it meant a new religious order. Something must be done.' In the same letter, he manifested a characteristic openness to new developments that would assist him as a confessor and moralist. He urged Columban to get a copy of a new book – *Moral Problems Now, Modern Techniques and Emotional Problems*, by George Hagmaier CSP and Robert W. Gleason SJ (England 1959) – which he described as a 'must'.[213]

Returning once again to Colonel Cave, it appears that Eugene received letters from him regularly. While Eugene excused himself as a bad correspondent, he did in fact write a number of letters in reply. The four which remain are necessarily different in tone from those written to Flood, in that they are addressed to a student for the priesthood. Reflecting the assured authority for which Eugene was noted, they included spiritual advice and direction.[214] He confirmed for Cave that he was not imagining his vocation, and that he had a vocation 'to try to become a priest in the Sudan'. He further assured him, 'Past history has nothing to do with your future except, perhaps, as a reminder of how complete is one's need of God's constant grace, and how essential *union with God* is for *you* in any walk of life.'

On 19 November 1950, Eugene sympathised with Cave on his difficulties with Latin and Philosophy at the Beda College, suggesting that he might employ someone to give him a few hours each week on the Latin text. He warned him about identifying

---

212 'Eugene's Letter 1961', 3 Nov. 1961, MSJA. Written to Magdalen who later sent it to Fr Nivard.
213 Eugene to Columban, 12 Feb. 1961. 'Correspondence File 1964–1969', MSJA. Fr Nivard to Columban, 17 Nov. 1964, MJSA.
214 Eugene to Col. Cave, 14 Oct. 1949, 10 Nov. 1950, 6 May 1951, 10 & 14 May 1952, MSJA.

the priesthood with pastoral activities, and referred him to chapter fifteen of St John's Gospel, where there is scarcely a word about activity, but a reminder 'that the *only* way to bring forth fruit is to abide in Him.' And he added practically, 'It is not necessary to strain for recollection all day, but a moment's thought and a return to Him now and then will do a lot to keep one in touch with Him', adding that 'God is far more interested in keeping in touch with you, than you can realise.'

In the New Year, on 8 January 1951, Eugene wrote to sympathise with Cave on the death of his father, saying that he had offered Mass for him. Had he known of his death he might have been able to attend the funeral, because he had been in London around the same time. He went on to remind Cave of 'one great fundamental principle – that the will of God is our sanctification and that in the work of our sanctification (which means uniting us to Himself) God is bound by no rules. He can and does use anything as the means of giving us grace and uniting us to Himself.' Eugene reminded him once more of chapters thirteen to fifteen of St John's Gospel. Some months later, On 6 May, Eugene in a brief note to Cave expressed thanks for the letters he had received, and said that he was looking forward to his visit to Roscrea.

A year later, on 10 May 1952, Eugene again expressed thanks for the letters he had received from Cave and also for the draft of a sermon he had sent, which Eugene assured him was 'excellent'. Writing on 15 May, Eugene emphasised that it was of the highest importance for him, in his preparation for the priesthood, to get a good understanding of the meaning of the Mass. He then developed a theme that occurred in others of his letters:

> The ordinary textbook treatment of the Mass has been spoiled by a wrong emphasis in the discussion of sacrifice. The writers of the past few centuries tend to stress the destruction of the victim and to make the destruction the essential part of the sacrifice. The same idea is carried into the spiritual life. Luckily recent years have brought out a few writers who have got back to the old authors and who

realise that to sacrifice is primarily to 'make holy'. This is
important, because I feel that the essential preparation for
the priesthood and the essential spirit for its performance
is the spirit of sacrifice – and by that I mean the continual
will to give oneself generously to God and so be made holy.

In the liturgy of the Mass, Eugene continued, 'as soon as the
Church starts to offer sacrifice (at the offering of the bread and
wine) she immediately prays that the Holy Ghost may come and
sanctify what she is offering. This is of capital importance. It is
by the Holy Ghost that we offer ourselves and are made holy ...
Our work is merely to dispose ourselves and remove outstanding
obstacles so that the Holy Spirit may have a free hand in our souls
and in all our works.' He then added, 'Our Lord insisted that he
was "sanctifying" Himself for *us* ... A priest must do the same ...
sanctify himself for his flock.'

Eugene's personal and direct approach arises from his reflection
on experience and mirrors his reading. It was particularly marked
several years later in a letter he wrote from Caldey to his sister,
just before her final profession as a Cistercian in 1955. He moved
straightaway to the basic elements of religious life.

I know all the dying involved in being a Cistercian ... If we
give ourselves to God completely, we have to follow Our
Lord on his *via crucis* – and there's no meaning in being a
Cistercian unless we see it as a means of giving ourselves to
Him and replacing ourselves by Him ... Our life is merely
a fulfilling of the sacrifice of ourselves we make with and
in Christ at the Mass ... One thing I insist upon. Every
failure in the spiritual life can be traced back to a *lack of
confidence*. As I wrote (in T.L.) – the reason for our hope in
God is *God's* goodness, not ours, so that there is no limit to
our hope. It must never be narrowed by *any* considerations
of our self.' [215]

---

215 Eugene to Magdalen, 1955, MSJA. An extract sent to Fr Nivard.
(T.L. = *Tremendous Lover*).

DOWN-TO-EARTH CONSOLATION

Eugene's retreatants, and others who came to him for spiritual guidance, are likely to have received the same kind of down-to-earth, consoling advice he gave to his own mother. Adapting his message to her busy life and outgoing personality, it was yet all of a piece with the wider teaching he gave in his books and conferences. He began with three texts from scripture: 'Your Father who is in heaven knoweth you have need of those things' (Mt 6:8), 'Thou shalt call his name Jesus for he shall save ...' (Mt 1:21) and 'Christ is all in all' (Col 3:11). Then he continued:

> Nothing, absolutely nothing, happens that Our Father has not willed or permitted, and in all that, he is perfectly fulfilling his part as Christ's Father and ours, so that everything that happens, even your own sins, to say nothing of infidelities, is designed for your transformation in Christ. Secondly, no matter how you sin, how you fail, what you do, Jesus, the Son of God, is waiting to be your Saviour, to undo all the wrong you have done. To do all the things you have left undone, and to complete all the good you have done badly. He is your 'supplement'. Finally, everything that you come in contact with is in some way or other Christ. That, of course, has to be understood properly. But, for example, the foolish gardener who delays you with some foolish complaint, the various tradesmen who can be so annoying etc., in dealing with all these you are dealing with Christ ... He comes to us in tattered garments of human foolishness but wants to be dealt with as he has a right.

'That, I think,' Eugene adds unexpectedly, 'is where a superior can only find Christ, in all that she meets in the daily round.'

Moving towards his third text, Eugene speaks with even more encouragement:

> These hectic days of yours, my dear Mother, these many cares that must be a plague, they all bring you Jesus,

perhaps even more certainly than Holy Communion. They are the actions of God's Paternity, of Jesus our Saviour, and they are the formation of Christ, in whom God is so well pleased, in you. Cast your cares upon the Lord and he will do *all* because he intends to restore *all* things in Christ who is *all in all.* No matter what *we* do, we are unprofitable servants. Therefore, let us do what seems best and leave the rest to God. And even if we fail to do that, let us accept it, acknowledge our meanness, and there is thus born a new measure of humility which gives more room for Christ.[216]

Little wonder that Eugene's teaching brought such a positive reaction from his numerous readers and hearers. It conveyed a wonderfully positive and consoling message in an era when preaching and theology tended to portray God as principally concerned with duty and retribution.

To conclude this chapter, where we got a glimpse of Eugene, the friend and spiritual advisor, discussing matters of common interest with his correspondents, it is informative to go back to some of the notes on prayer he wrote much earlier, before he had published any books. Keeping in mind how distracting his lifestyle would become later, it is striking what he had to say about St Benedict's teaching on prayer:

As to the practice of prayer: short and frequent ejaculations are about the best. One must keep one's convictions alive by daily spiritual reading done meditatively, and perhaps a little meditation ... For the rest, the great thing is to remember that the prayer of Christ at the right hand of God is The real prayer, and all our prayers must be united with that. So that every act of religion or of love which unites us to Christ, especially when we do the will of God, makes us participators in that prayer of His. If

---

216 Eugene to his mother, MSJA. No date, but typed sheets on 'Prayer', in close proximity to this text, are dated 6 Nov. 1937.

words help, use them. If they don't, don't worry. One's heart speaks. [217]

One wonders if this was the form of prayer Eugene used himself in order to keep in touch with his monastic vocation during his time in Australia, when he was far from the ambience and routine of Cistercian life. He may well have come back to it again during the months of travel and conferences that were ahead of him in the US.

217 Typed notes headed 'Prayer' 6/11/1937, MSJA.

CHAPTER 10

AN AMERICAN INTERLUDE, 1960

Shortly after his return to Roscrea from Caldey, Eugene obtained permission to go to the US in response to a request from some American Cistercian abbots to preach their annual retreat. Since he was writing for certain American magazines at the same time, the editors invited him to give conferences to priests as well.[218] He also realised that it was likely that other religious would invite him to give their annual retreats when they heard of his coming. All of this promised to bring in welcome income to Mount St Joseph Abbey. Eugene's visit was also welcomed by the publishers and distributers of his books. Incidentally, during his time in America Eugene sent several contributions to assist the monks at Notre Dame, Tarrawarra.[219]

Eugene appears to have moved from one monastery to another belonging to the Cistercians – or Trappists, as they are known in the US – as well as going out to give retreats, conferences and lectures to other religious, clergy and Catholic groups. There is only a limited amount of material available in Mount St Joseph about his movements in the US. A reference he made early on to contacts he had on Fifth Avenue in relation to the sale of perfume, suggests that he probably began his visit to North America in the New York area. It seems that he soon moved into the interior of the country in response to requests. It is clear that at one point he went to Seattle on the invitation of Fr William Treacy, assistant chancellor of the Archdiocese. Fr Treacy came from Roscrea and, many years previously, had met Eugene at Mount St Joseph

INTERVIEW IN SEATTLE

While in Seattle, Eugene was interviewed by Virginia Scott on behalf of a local paper, *The Progress*.[220] She announced that he was

218 Kinsella, *Dom Eugene Boylan*, p. 17.
219 Claffey, 'Profiles in Sanctity', p. 33, MSJA.
220 Local Newspaper, 4 March 1960. Among newspaper cuttings in the MSJ Archive.

the author of several widely-read books dealing with the spiritual life, which were appreciated by priests, religious and laity. The best known of these books, she told her readers, were *Difficulties in Mental Prayer, Spirituality for the Priest* and, of course, *This Tremendous Lover.* About the last-mentioned book, she stated that it was 'written especially for the laity' and that 'more than 100,000 copies have been sold'. During the week he spent in Seattle, Eugene's programme was evidently a full one. The article in *The Progress* noted that 'while in Seattle, Father Eugene will conduct a retreat for the Religious of the Sacred Heart at Forrest Ridge Convent and lecture to students at St Thomas seminary. The Knights of St Columbus (*sic*) and their friends will have an opportunity to hear Father Eugene on Monday, 7 March, at 8.00 p.m., at the K. C. Hall. "Spirituality for the Laity" will be the topic of his address.' On that theme he is quoted as saying that the 'Communists have given men an ideology that completely permeates their lives', and that 'the spiritualisation of the ordinary day's work of the ordinary lay person is the only practical answer to Communism'.

He was happy to range freely during his interview with Scott. He believed that, 'generally, the spiritual life of Catholics is growing at a rapid rate'. In discussing the Church in England, he thought that 'it is the thing to be a Catholic in London. Many intellectuals, members of the aristocracy, and theatre people were exhibiting interest in the Catholic Church.' He mentioned Princess Margaret's interest in Catholicism and praised Queen Elizabeth, 'particularly for her work against Communism'. On America, he confessed, 'I really know nothing about America, since I've spent most of my time inside four monasteries since I've been here.' That did not stop him, however, from commenting that 'America has a much more virile Church than we have'. The great increase in vocations, he believed, was an indication of spiritual growth, and he pointed out that 'twelve years ago there were three Trappist monasteries in the United States. Now there are twelve, including the two largest monasteries in the world at Gethsemane, Kentucky, and Spencer, Massachusetts. Men from all walks of life and from all parts of the country are living in the monasteries.'

Insisting that 'prayer is the reason for vocations', Eugene believed that the great growth that had taken place in the aftermath of the Second World War was a result 'of the Family Rosary'. It is of interest to note that among the Trappist monasteries in which Eugene gave retreats was Gethsemane, which is associated in the popular mind with Thomas Merton. Merton is reported to have described Eugene's retreat as the best he had ever attended.

The interviewer for *The Progress* provided a brief verbal sketch of Father Eugene's family, commenting that he had 'a brother who is prior of the newly-established Carthusian monastery in Vermont; a sister who is a Trappist in Ireland; and a sister who belongs to the Mary Reparatrice Sisters and is stationed in Cincinnati. Another brother and his 82-year-old mother live in Ireland. His father died many years ago.' Speaking of the one thing to which he might attribute his own vocation, Eugene revealed that 'other than a good Catholic home, it was the quiet devotion of my father'. The interviewer went on to give a summary of Eugene's career, before adding this paean:

> Pioneer, nuclear-physicist, mathematician, musician, author, discoverer of a formula for making perfume, lecturer, retreat master, confessor, Trappist superior – Fr Eugene is all of these. Fr Treacy sums him up in one word – 'genius'. Fr Eugene is a genial genius with a keen sense of humour. He is a humble man.

CONFLICT IN KANSAS CITY

Eugene's reception at his next port of call was a more sober experience. He stayed for two days at the well laid-out 'Paris of the Plains', Kansas City, where he was too well-known as author and lecturer to pass unnoticed. Patricia Jansen Doyle, a reporter for the *Kansas City Star*, met with him and commented that he was in the city on a two-day rest 'from a speaking-tour of Trappist monasteries'. Then, having given something of his background, her interview was highlighted with a bold headline – 'Caldy (*sic*) Trappists Blend Perfume for

Livelihood'. It was a heading that caught the attention of the bishop of the diocese of Kansas City-Saint Joseph, the Most Rev. John P. Cody, and displeased him. Cody was already displeased that Eugene was operating in his diocese without his permission, and he had his Chancellor, Mgr Joseph V. Sullivan, send the following lengthy message to Eugene's Abbot in Roscrea, Dom Camillus Claffey:

> On March 12, 1960, the Chancery Office learned indirectly that the Revd M. Eugene Boylan OCSO had given a Triduum to Sisters of the Convent of the Sacred Heart, St Joseph, Missouri, and had subsequently given a conference to the Sisters of the House of the Good Shepherd, Kansas City, Missouri, without the proper faculties of the Diocese.

Sullivan then pointed out that it was the established practice in the Diocese that

> faculties for religious are sought through their religious superior. In the case above, faculties were not requested by anyone, and none were granted. This was a serious situation since the confessions of religious women were heard. Father Boylan was invited to the Chancery Office to give an explanation. It appears there was confusion in Father's mind. He did not know that St Joseph, Missouri, was in the diocese of Kansas City-Saint Joseph, and he had presumed that since he was invited by the Mother Superior of the convent to give a Triduum that faculties had been secured.

The Chancellor then went on to say that his Excellency, Bishop Cody, 'would have been most happy to grant the faculties if they had been requested', and elaborated further:

> The Kansas City area is predominantly non-Catholic and the local press occasionally publish bizarre items concerning the Church which are embarrassing. Because of this, the Bishop required that any publicity released to the press by churches or Catholic institutions should be handled by the Chancery. Father Boylan was in Kansas

City, and without the knowledge of his Excellency, an interview was given by him to a reporter concerning a perfume produced by the Trappist Monks in Wales. It received a front-page coverage and has been a source of considerable amusement in the area, and the overall effects of the press release were not desirable.

On a partly conciliatory note, the Chancellor concluded, 'His Excellency did not wish to occasion any difficulty for Father Boylan. Presumably he intended no embarrassment to anyone, but to prevent any similar situations from arising, which might injure your good relations with the Dioceses of the United States, His Excellency thought these matters ought to be brought to your attention.'[221] Mgr. Sullivan enclosed a copy of the press release that had appeared in the *Kansas City Star* on 23 March, 1960.

DEMANDS FOR HIS SERVICES

A similar lack of sensitivity towards the local situation arose in Eugene's relationship with some Trappist monasteries in the United States. On at least one occasion, Eugene advertised in a clerical magazine that he was available to give lectures, conferences and retreats. This initiative led some of the American abbots to write to Claffey in Roscrea requesting that Eugene be recalled, as he was replacing some of their own men who were doing the same work.[222]

Eugene continued giving retreats and conferences in the United States. On 29 June 1960, he wrote to Claffey concerning income from his recent retreats. 'These five retreats', he reported, 'should bring in at least another $1,000', and he estimated the whole American trip would bring in about $1,700, although 'the travelling expenses here will have eaten up part of that'.[223] There was no decline in the demand for his services. 'All the bishops are asking for return visits. I have refused to make any promises' because 'since 27 January I've

221 Boylan Papers, USA Trip 5/5/1 no. 13, MSJA; and Mgr. V. Sullivan to Dom Claffey, 7 April 1960, 5/5/7 no. 5, MSJA.
222 Kinsella, *Dom Eugene Boylan*, p. 17.
223 Eugene to Claffey, 29 June 1960, 5/4, MSJA.

had about seven free days altogether.'[224] In October, he informed Claffey that in addition to requests from religious and ecclesiastics for lectures, he had also received a request from a university. He had been invited 'to give a course of 13 lectures in the University of Notre Dame to religious on "The Nature and Sources of Ascetic Theology". I had to refuse, as without a library, without sufficient time to prepare, I could not have done it other than superficially.'[225]

In her interview with Eugene in the *Kansas City Star*, Patricia Jansen Doyle asked him why he had left science for religious life. 'That's a difficult question', he replied, and then went on to cover familiar ground in his answer: 'Perhaps looking for something better to do – something better in life. When a man joins the Trappists he must do so for more than a mere sense of duty. He must have a personal ideal, a wish for a personal relationship with God'.

In the same interview, he described his visit to the United States 'as just giving pep talks', and he refuted the suggestion that he was 'a trouble shooter for the Trappists'. When asked his views on John F. Kennedy's candidacy for the presidency of the US, Eugene did not hesitate in his response. 'Religion should have nothing to do with it', he asserted, 'but if you will forgive me, a guest in this country, I don't believe the American public is mature enough for a Catholic President.' This response may well have contributed to Bishop Cody's embarrassment at Eugene's presence.

Eugene was open about his views on both political and religious life, but at times was he was more forthcoming with his opinions than diplomacy would dictate. He was, as his friends on Caldey had remarked, 'too straight'. He could be equally forthcoming with his views on the Church in Ireland, and on political and economic life there too.

---

224 Eugene to Claffey, 29 June 1960, 5/4, MSJA.
225 Eugene to Claffey, 26 Oct. 1960, 5/4, MSJA.

CHAPTER 11

POLITICAL, RELIGIOUS, SOCIAL AND ECONOMIC VIEWS

As a young man, Eugene showed a keen interest in politics. His inaugural address to the Literary and Historical Society in University College Dublin, in 1926, was entitled 'Democracy and Fundamental Principles'. In it he questioned the formula 'one man, one vote' as sufficient for expressing the ideal of democracy. He argued that it did not ensure the achievement of results arising from wise, informed opinion. In the absence of practical means of determining an individual's fitness to vote, he argued, the formula was taken by political movements as the only practical application of democracy that safeguards civil, religious and individual liberty.[226] His interest in politics in those years was such that some people were pressing him to start a Catholic political party.[227]

IRELAND'S MISSION TO THE WORLD
Three years later, in 1929, in an article in the O'Connell School magazine, his emphasis was on Christianising the new Ireland. He envisaged the country as having a mission to give a lead to other countries by being both Irish and Catholic, directed by Catholic social and religious principles, and bringing God back into politics and business. 'The situation is urgent', he wrote. 'If we in Ireland do not cultivate a completely Catholic outlook, if we do not learn to judge everything by Catholic principles alone, if we do not rise above "the spirit of the time", then Ireland has failed in her mission, and Europe has lost one of its future leaders.'[228]

A similar spirit is manifested in an undated document entitled 'Industrialization', written perhaps during the 1930s under the Fianna Fáil Government. In that text, Eugene referred to new

---

226 The inaugural address to L & H. Society, UCD, no date, 5/5/5, no. 1, MSJA.
227 Dom Columban Mulcahy in interview with Fr Nivard.
228 Eugene's article 'Our Task' in the school magazine, 5/5/1, no.1, MSJA.

industries being introduced into Ireland on the initiative of the government. He observes that 'to the extent that these should be the natural basis for supernatural growth[229] they are clearly to be welcomed, but unless such gains helped spiritual growth, and were not merely progress on a material plane, then experience suggests that it is likely to be harmful'.[230] Eugene's extant comments on industrial and social development are sparse.

POLITICAL CONCERNS

As has been noted already, the 1930s brought political division, economic hardship and strong criticism of the government by some bishops, including Dr Fogarty, bishop of the diocese of Killaloe, in whose diocese Roscrea is situated. The monks, especially those active in church work, were aware of such developments in the country. They were aware of other developments too – the swell of opinion supporting Franco in the Spanish Civil War, and the support for Irish neutrality as another world war loomed.

In 1942, American troops landed in Northern Ireland. In March 1943, Francis Spellman, archbishop of New York, came to Ireland on a private mission from the American president to persuade de Valera to join the forces of civilisation against the Axis powers. Spellman hoped to win over the Irish bishops to his side, but failed. After the war, he made a pronouncement critical of Irish neutrality and particularly of the Irish ports not being made available to the Allies. The issues in question arose at a time of tension between Britain and Ireland over partition, while at the same time relations between Ireland and the US were also strained.

Eugene was clearly interested. He sought the opinion of someone, whose identity we do not know but whose views he clearly respected, asking his opinion of the 'Memorandum regarding the Irish Ports and the letter to Cardinal Spellman'. The reply ran to several pages. The writer displayed a detailed knowledge of modern

229 The thinking appears to be that people in improved material circumstances have more opportunity for religious practice.
230 Document on industrialisation, 5/5/1, no. 11, MSJA.

Irish history and of past difficulties in negotiating with England. He ridiculed America and England being termed the forces of Christian civilisation, and he emphasised that America had no right to complain about Irish neutrality, seeing that she herself observed neutrality until attacked by the Japanese. It seems that the well-versed writer was a local man, since much of his document was written on the back of paper headed 'Roscrea Co-Operative Creamery Ltd.'. This exchange might indicate that Eugene was involved in some active local discussion on national and international affairs.

CONCERN FOR THE IRISH CHURCH

In 1947 Eugene was very concerned again about the social and spiritual reform of society. He wrote an article for the magazine *Christus Rex,* entitled 'The Priest, Social Studies and Spirituality', which appeared in October that year. In it he sought to make the values of the papal social encyclicals, joined to a deeper interior life, a reality in society. To lead this crusade, in the absence of an educated Catholic leisured class in Ireland, the priests were the natural leaders. 'It is our business', he wrote in summary, 'to labour that Christ be formed in all things. Our adversaries have chosen the structures of society as the battle ground. There we must meet their attack. A Christian social organisation is at once the result of Christ's life in the members of society, and also a means to form Christ in them. We priests have responsibility for the life of "the whole Christ". To fulfil that duty we must first bring forth Christ in individual souls, and then bring forth Christ in society; but we must also remember that the Christianisation of public life is one of the very best means of ensuring the Christianising of public life. And we must start with ourselves. We must make ourselves competent guides in social matters.'

This meant that priests needed to be trained as sociologists, or to be highly informed on social matters, and to have a strong interior life as well, if the crusade were to be effective. The problem was that both bishops and Government showed no great interest, and the clergy themselves were less than enthusiastic. Two years later, Eugene privately expressed himself highly critical of priests and bishops in the Irish church. As already mentioned, his letter to Dom Peter Flood, written on 16 December 1949, criticised the 'conventional inertia' of the Irish Church and endorsed the critical comments in the *Irish Ecclesiastical Record* about the relations between clergy and people in France as applicable to Ireland. He himself, he wrote, had fired his first shots 'in the attack on the clerical problem in Ireland' by publishing in book form some articles he had first written for American readers.[231]

Eugene's concern about the relationship between clergy and people was to be reinforced in 1960 following correspondence with the redoubtable and independent-minded parish priest, John Fennelly. On 23 October 1960, Fennelly informed Eugene that he had spent 'an interesting and refreshing two weeks roaming the South, listening and probing into the problem of the Church and people of Ireland in our day.' He 'spoke to the laity and encouraged them to speak their minds', and his general conclusion was that the Church was losing its grip on the social and daily life of the people.

In hindsight, many of Fennelly's observations were remarkably perceptive. 'Ordinary folk', he reported, 'retain a regard for their faith, for Christian moral standards, but they are ill-instructed' and unacquainted with the Church's views on the social and spiritual problems of the age. 'Ecclesiastical standards are low and folk do not read anything worthwhile about religion. They are starving for the word of God and waiting for invitation into the liturgy of the Church. The clergy remain aloof and complacent, not making any attempt to study the people or the problems of the Church of the time. Religion tends to become a mere Sunday business, a duty … in the most perfunctory way (by priest and people) and forgotten for the rest of the week. Anti-clericalism is rumbling underneath … and is in danger of breaking point and wrecking the whole Church.'[232]

Eugene's concern for the diocesan clergy found expression in

---

231 Eugene to Peter Flood, 16 Dec. 1949, 'Individual Letters', 5/5/1, no. 12, MSJA. The articles in *I.E.R.* vol. 72, July–Dec. 1949, were by Father Stephen Roche and entitled 'The Priest life in France'.
232 John Fennelly to Eugene, 26 Oct. 1960, 5/5/1, no. 1 (House History ch. 5), MSJA.

several ways: the conferences devoted to them; his availability on a personal level in Roscrea; his encouragement and instruction in his book *The Spiritual Life of the Priest* (1949); and his final work *The Priest's Way to God,* published in 1962.

FURTHER POLITICAL AND ECONOMIC CONCERNS

The 1950s were marked by economic depression in Ireland, and thousands of Irish citizens emigrated to Britain and Canada in search of employment. Eugene welcomed technological development and increased industrialisation as ways of improving people's living standards, but not at the expense of spiritual growth. He felt, indeed, that improved living standards should afford opportunity for greater religious devotion. By 1961, he was in correspondence with Joseph Foyle, a Catholic economist and idealist. Foyle argued that people had a right to higher living standards but, given the country's limited resources and the large number of unemployed, that this was not attainable. In the circumstances, he argued, it seemed appropriate to promote increased emigration in order to provide fitting living standards for those remaining. To accomplish this without discrimination, it was necessary that certain canons be established to avoid the traditional use of 'influence'. When Eugene seemed to pull back from the conclusion of this argument, Foyle remarked that he, Boylan, did not 'have stomach' for the argument.

Eugene, indeed, was feeling depressed at the apparent apathy of Irish people. He believed that the Church should be actively involved with the laity in that time of change in Ireland, and that religion should be part of the daily working life. On 7 October 1960, a newspaper report referred to a lecture of his to the Catholic Association under the heading 'Revision of Ideals Advocated'. Eugene is quoted as saying that 'unless we can find an ideal that will lead to co-operation and to a sense of our responsibility as citizens, state control – in an ever-increasing measure – is inevitable. The problem of inducing every citizen to live and work for the national good must be solved, whether by a totalitarian state or by the properly understood ideal of Christian society.'

COMBINING ECONOMIC AND SPIRITUAL GROWTH

In his final years, especially after his appointment as abbot, Eugene extolled the rural way of living as being more in tune with reflection and the spiritual life. He appears at that time to have been in wider communication with local farmers and their associations. He came up with a practical proposal for 'an industry most likely to bring economic prosperity to Ireland without disturbing the essentially sound structure of Irish religious and social life'. The industry proposed was 'the production, processing and packaging of food for export'.

> This would have the effect of taking Irish rural and semi-rural communities as they exist and raising their standard of living in matters of food, housing, schools, health services; and also providing work for a proportion of those who are at present compelled to seek it overseas. Outside business firms might be prepared to encourage and assist such an enterprise, if it were demonstrated that the will and the ability to make it a success are present. The development of this form of industry has the additional advantage of providing a more stable and healthy economy – as far as possible self-contained, self-sufficient – in a rapidly changing international economy. Other industries are already arising but the production of one's own food, with a surplus to export in return for less essential goods, is likely to produce a happier economy than one that depends on the export of manufactured goods with a fluctuating market to the neglect of agriculture.

He went on to show how, in his view, the proposal could serve as a real means of combining economic and spiritual growth:

> If the economic revival that could be effected by this were linked with the spiritual renewal that recent Popes, from Pius X on, have urged and hoped to see as a result of a fuller participation of the laity in the public worship of the Church and a deeper understanding of the Church

and her sacraments and round of feasts, then the two could go hand in hand and reinforce the other. In fact, such an economy, traditional in Ireland, rooted in the soil and based on a community small enough for everyone to have an obvious stake in it and to observe all that is going on, is the ideal one for helping towards this deeper penetration of the life of the Church in the Mass, the Office, and Sacraments, and the 'matter' and symbolism of the sacraments, presuppose a familiarity at first hand with the seasons of the year and the accomplishment of seasonal tasks, observation of the phenomena of nature as they can be seen most fully only in the countryside, the immediate production of food and the basic necessities of life.

'In short,' Eugene asserts, 'there should be, ideally, an essential interaction between economic and spiritual growth – and Ireland still has the conditions in which this could be achieved.'

Eugene then goes on to address the practicalities of his proposal.

The practical question is how best to introduce a scheme for such an integral renewal of life proceeding at one and the same time on natural and supernatural levels. It is suggested that it would be advisable to start on a small scale with one model or 'pilot' community as a pattern for the rest. People could come and see it working, and when the demand arose it could be duplicated elsewhere. If it proved successful, then each unit would tend to inspire others and it would spread. The parish is normally the next unit after the family, and perhaps the most effective way to begin would be to find an especially energetic and knowledgeable parish priest, who had an appreciation of all the issues involved and was in a position to carry out as closely as possible this approach to recovery through rural life informed by a deeper understanding and practice of religion, and work with him.

'It is important', Eugene cautioned, 'to start with a practical plan at the outset, beginning small and working steadily, if only with a single household, or better a "depressed" village with undeveloped potentialities.' Finally, drawing to a conclusion this practical reflection on aspects of rural development, he observed that 'these days we are feeling our way towards a fuller synthesis of material and spiritual, and such a movement, with proper guidance, is capable of transforming from within the prevalent materialism and secularism that threaten society.'[233] Eugene did not live to see the major impact of food processing on Irish rural life. In a more secular Ireland, it took the form of big and competitive business linked to giant creameries, with little indication of his desired 'synthesis of the material and spiritual'.

PRACTICAL INVOLVEMENT

After his appointment as abbot in 1962, Eugene displayed a down-to-earth approach to the monastery's farming requirements and to local needs. Thus, he became actively engaged in supporting a proposal 'by 322 farmers in our neighbourhood for a cream-separation station in Shinrone' – a village midway between Roscrea and Nenagh. On 9 November, he wrote to the Taoiseach about the matter. The Nenagh Creamery Board, he explained, had already agreed to the proposal (in preference to a proposal from Birr) and they were applying to the Irish Agricultural Organisation Society in order to bring the matter further. He had been told that the proposal might run counter to Government policy of fewer and bigger creameries. He went on to point out, however, that even that policy 'will have to solve the problem of transport costs to the factory, which could be done by the use of such local cream-separating stations as here proposed.'

Eugene then went on to draw on the experience of the monastery farm. Shinrone 'offers us an average distance of transport of 5.35 miles against our present average of 14.65 miles (Birr would be about 12–14 miles)'. He pointed out that 'the transport cost is one great obstacle to the profitable production of milk, and the establishment of the station at Shinrone would facilitate the government policy of

233 Document on industrialisation, 5/5/1, no. 11, MSJA.

increasing the cattle population, which policy we are trying to put into effect.' He assured the taoiseach that 'any help that can be given to the proposal would be deeply appreciated'.

Eugene backed up his letter with a list of the 322 farmers who, he said, 'offer 1,400,000 gallons of milk per year if Nenagh creamery establish a separating-station at Shinrone'. Comparing the possible locations, he claimed that only Shinrone 'can produce a worthwhile reduction in transport distance'. Moreover, separating-stations such as the one proposed reduce transport costs and 'can supply central butter factories established in accordance with Government policy'. 'Only such a scheme', he claimed, 'can facilitate the farmers here in carrying out Government policy of increasing cattle population.' Not surprisingly, such support for local interests added to the high reputation Eugene already enjoyed in the Roscrea region as preacher, confessor – and abbot.

PART III: 1960–64

CHAPTER 12

HOME FOR GOOD, 1960–64

On his return to Roscrea from the US, Eugene found himself busy but happy. He was active in the monastery's public church – celebrating Mass, preaching and hearing confessions – and 'he was often called on to preach weekend retreats at the guesthouse and give the diocesan priests a day of recollection'.[234]

On 12 February 1961, he responded to Columban Mulcahy in Nunraw, who had requested him to conduct their annual retreat. Having received permission to do so, Eugene in his reply spoke openly about himself. 'I find myself taking up a very definite line in spirituality and speaking with certainty even authority. Yet the contrast between what I teach and what I am makes me wonder whether there isn't a mistake somewhere. So I'll be glad to get a "check-up" on my ideas'.

Eugene then went on to list his many activities in a manner that might seem boastful in anybody else. 'Apart from the fact that I have been acting as Father Master (of novices) for over six weeks (Fr Master was ill), and that I give the Brothers two conferences every week, I had to take on the Pastoral Theology (class) at short notice. *Faute de mieux,* I started off on Spirituality – giving more or less "my" retreat, and found that half the priests in the house were dropping in.' Eugene then remarked frankly, that while there was little to report generally from Mount St Joseph, 'for myself, I'm more happy than I have been for years. I'm even beginning to say my prayers and not to want to do anything else (I needn't say, my prayers are very much *sui generis*).' He added that he had represented the Abbot at a meeting of major religious superiors. His presence, he

234 Claffey, 'Profiles in Sanctity', p. 33, MSJA.

thought, was largely 'to give me a chance of seeing my mother. Her heart is "wonky" and she must take it easy'. Finally, he wondered about the forthcoming General Council of the Church and what it might achieve. 'I'm wondering is there any chance of getting the next Council to restate the fundamentals of the religious life. They are being overlooked. Secondly, can no better provision be made for the spiritual direction of women (especially nuns)? Even if it meant a new religious order, something must be done.'[235]

THE DEATH OF EUGENE'S MOTHER

Mrs Boylan's 'wonky' heart was perhaps in a more serious condition than Eugene realised or his mother wished him to know. When she died on 9 May 1961, her death left a large gap in his life. His sense of loss was tempered somewhat by the public tributes to her as a person and as a musician. One newspaper spoke of the passing of 'the Grand Old Lady of Irish musical education' who had 'the special gift of leading by kindness and affection, which inspired the loyalty and confidence of her pupils ... In the wider field of Irish music she had an established place. A gifted performer herself, she was at home in all branches of musical art but particularly expert in the field of choral singing'.[236]

Despite the strict rules of enclosure, Eugene received permission to be with his mother before she died. This was a consolation to him and to his brothers and sisters. On 5 June, 1961, his sister Molly wrote to him from her convent in Cincinnati, Ohio:

> You have no idea how much I thanked God that you were there at the end – because nothing could have given Mama more joy. You could do for her what none of us could have done ... and it was also a help to poor Gerald to have you with him.[237]

Gerald had not only taken care of his mother during her illness; at the same time he was caring for his wife who was suffering

235 Eugene to Abbot of Nunraw, 12 Feb. 1961, MSJA. Letter given to Fr Nivard by Dom Columban Mulcahy on 17 Nov. 1964.
236 Newspaper cutting in MSJA, but title of newspaper missing.
237 Molly to Eugene, 5 June 1961, 5/3/1, MSJA.

from terminal cancer, and who would die later that same year. Not surprisingly, his brothers and sisters viewed him as the holiest member of the family.[238]

His mother's death probably interfered with some of Eugene's commitments. His retreat at Nunraw was delayed, so that he did not return from there to Roscrea until mid-December. In a letter written on 21 December 1961 to Fr Marius McAuliffe OFM, an old friend of his, Eugene explained that he had just come home from Nunraw, and he apologised for keeping his book so long. He would be sending it back to him after Christmas.

Then, in his direct way, Eugene told McAuliffe that he had reacted against one idea in the book. The author had implied that failure to comply with a particular grace from God would result in the person being lost forever. This, said Eugene, was 'not a true picture of God's action. It neither reflects God's mercy nor does it do justice to the completeness of Our Lord's *saving* action'. After further reflections on God's grace and his often slow ways, Eugene referred to a text from an old calendar which had caught his attention and reflected his own belief. 'It was from St Bernard: "For merit, it suffices to know that our own merits do not suffice".' He then went on, 'I gave it to Dom Malachy, the retired abbot of Mount St Bernard (Leicestershire, England) who is at Nunraw, and had been my first novice-master. He seemed to think it meant a lot.'[239] Dom Malachy's considered views were important to Eugene.

ELECTION AS ABBOT

When Dom Camillus Claffey offered his resignation to the Abbot General early in 1962, the prospect of a major change caused uncertainty in Mount St Joseph. In response to his resignation, Claffey received word that his resignation would not be accepted until after Easter, because of the absence of so many in Rome at the time. The election of a successor was delayed until 10 July 1962. It is not clear what Eugene's expectations were as the day of

238 Claffey, 'Profiles in Sanctity', p. 26, MSJA.
239 Eugene to Marius McAuliffe, OFM, 21 Dec. 1961, MSJA.

election drew near, but the special chapter, which began at 8.30 in the morning, eventually elected him as abbot by a narrow majority. 'After the fifth scrutiny, the senior scrutator, Fr Patrick, announced that Dom Eugene Boylan had received the required majority of votes and he was proclaimed fourth Abbot of Mount St Joseph.' Eugene then gave his consent to the office which, in the words of the Ritual is 'a burden which would break the back of an angel'. On the completion of all the formalities, there was a short break before the office of Sext was recited at the usual time – 12.47pm.[240]

The electors were required to keep the result confidential until the result was approved by the Abbot General, and so the new abbot occupied an ordinary rank in the choir. The brothers and the non-voting choir members were left to guess at the result, but most of them seemed to guess correctly. On the afternoon of the election, Dom Camillus Claffey went to Dublin by car, hoping to have the election papers speedily transmitted to Rome via the nunciature's diplomatic bag. He informed the Abbot General by telephone that the summary of the act of election was on its way.[241] Confirmation of Eugene's election was received by telephone from the abbot general's office on the morning of Wednesday, 11 July, and shortly afterwards the High Mass – the votive Mass of St Joseph – was offered in thanksgiving for the election and for the intentions of Dom Eugene. After the office of None, in accordance with the Ritual, Eugene was installed as Abbot by the 'Father Immediate' – in this case Dom Finbarr Cashman, Abbot of Mount Melleray, the mother house of Roscrea. Afterwards, the community went in procession to the church singing the *Te Deum*. Sometime later, all members of the community assembled outside for photographs, and the Irish television station, Telefís Éireann, was there to film the occasion for the public news.

That evening Abbot Eugene, accompanied by Dom Mulcahy, travelled to Dublin to fulfil a commitment, given some months earlier, to give a conference to a gathering of Major Religious

240 Monastery Chronicles, vol. 6 (Jan. 1960–10 Sept. 1973), 10 July 1963.
241 Monastery Chronicles.

Dom Eugene on the day of his abbatial blessing, 5th August 1962, with his brother, Gerald.

Superiors.[242] The following day, he gave an address to a Congress of Novice Mistresses at Eccles Street in Dublin. A sister who was present gave an enthusiastic account of his talk which conveyed something of his driving energy and conviction.

> Dom Eugene was magnificent ... The lecture was on the day following the Election and he had been 21 hours up, and so was not a little *exalté* – but the lecture was powerful. The reproduction which is about to appear in *Doctrine and Life* will really give no idea of the spoken word. He walked up and down and spoke for an hour and a quarter. It was the fruit of years and years of experience, and I found it wonderful.[243]

242 Monastery Chronicles.
243 Material on the appointment of Abbot Boylan, Grey box 11, MSJA.

IMMEDIATE REACTIONS

For the community in Roscrea, the memorable day of Eugene's installation concluded with them receiving permission to go to the college after Compline to see the report of the event on television. For many of them it was their first opportunity to watch television. On the next day, the monastery chronicle noted that 'extensive laudatory reports appeared in the Irish newspapers that morning, outlining Dom Eugene's career and announcing his election. Congratulatory telegrams and letters are pouring in.' On Friday, 13 July, the chronicler observed 'that a meeting was held in the Abbey Hall, Roscrea, at which it was decided that the townspeople of Roscrea would present Dom Eugene with his abbatial ring. The new abbot's election had been received with great joy in the neighbourhood. Dom Eugene will certainly be a popular abbot.'

On Saturday, a blackboard was erected in the cloister on which cuttings and photographs from the local and national press were posted, outlining the new abbot's career. 'For once,' the chronicler remarked tartly, 'the reporters seem to have got their facts right, and there were none of the usual blunders nor glamorised exaggerated statements.' That same afternoon, at about 5.15, Abbot Eugene returned to Mount St Joseph, and provided a foretaste of things to come. 'His boundless energy seemed to have him in ten places at once, as he went about the business of settling into the abbot's room and, of course, reading the multitude of greetings and good wishes.'[244]

INITIAL ADDRESS IN CHAPTER.

The next day, Sunday, 15 July, Eugene gave his first address in chapter as abbot. The Monastery Chronicle noted that he took as his text, 'Jesus Christ, yesterday, today, and the same forever' (Heb 13:8). 'Christ is the superior of the monastery', he said, 'and He makes His will known to us through the men he places over us – regardless of their abilities and qualities.' He asked that the prior see to it that the High Mass every Sunday be celebrated for

244 Monastery Chronicle, 14 July.

the spiritual and temporal needs of the community. Every priest, moreover, should celebrate Mass, one day a month, for his own spiritual needs and those of the community. The abbot would himself 'celebrate Mass for the community – or some individual need of a member of the community – every Sunday and three or four times per week'.

The chronicle goes on to say that Eugene 'spoke further of the abbot's position – because of his taking the place of Christ in our regard – as both head and saviour'. He first charged the community 'to show all honour to Abbot Camillus, whose simple faith, prayer and union with God had brought many blessings on us'. He then stated that in his new role he did not intend to be 'a policeman', and that anyone bearing tales would be asked by him, 'Have you prayed for Father or Brother So-and-So? Perhaps you are not praying enough.' As abbot, he would be 'completely at the disposal of the brethren, who should not be put off by his exterior'. He wished, however, 'that we should come quickly to the point, as long preambles hold up the work of getting things done'.

He then added that the bishop of the diocese, Most Revd Joseph Rodgers, would be present on Sunday, 5 August, to bless the new abbot. The ceremony (and celebrations) would be 'restricted to the community and some ecclesiastics' because 'the Abbot General does not wish large-scale banquets'. This was not meant to draw the line, however, if the general public were to be invited at a later date. Also, he added, small receptions 'may be held for select groups – viz. Roscrea and neighbours, past men of the school etc.'

Some members of the community were taken aback by Dom Eugene's comment about 'coming quickly to the point', as it seemed to suggest impatience and some restrictions on his availability. Nevertheless, as the Monastery Chronicle observed with relief:

> After the uncertainties of the past year, and the great speculations of the past few months, the community is again at peace. Once more we have a father in Christ. There is already a feeling of settling down again – things are becoming stable again. And there is both joy and

expectation on the threshold of this new reign – the reign of the Fourth Abbot of Mount St Joseph. AD MULTOS ANNOS!

THE ABBATIAL BLESSING

The blessing of a new abbot by the bishop, according to the Cistercian rite, is a detailed and solemn affair. According to the special booklet printed for the occasion, the abbot-elect is assisted in the ceremony by two other abbots. The bishop is met at the church door by the abbot-elect and some of the monks. A procession is then formed and proceeds to the High Altar, where some prayers are said. When the vesting of the bishop has taken place, he comes to the altar and the abbot-elect is presented to him. At this stage, the bishop, according to ancient tradition, addresses a series of interrogations to the future abbot. He questions him 'as to his intention of being faithful to his holy profession, of observing the Rule of St Benedict, and of seeing that his subjects observe it; of his intention to refrain from evil, and to tend to every good; to observe chastity, temperance, humility and patience, and of getting his subjects to do the same; of guarding faithfully the goods of the monastery; of devoting them to the service of the Church, the brethren, the poor and pilgrims, and of his subjection and obedience to the Holy Roman Church, and to the Sovereign Pontiff … as well as to his own immediate superior.'

When the abbot-elect 'has answered these interrogations affirmatively, the bishop supplicates Almighty God to bestow on him these and all other goods'. Then the abbot-elect , 'kneeling before the bishop with his hands on the Book of the Gospel, reads the form of the Oath in which he promises fidelity, subjection and obedience to the Mother House of the Order, to the Father Immediate, and to their successors, according to the constitutions of the Order'.[245] After this, the Mass takes place, during which the bishop imposes his hands on the head of the abbot-elect, praying 'that he who, by the imposition of our hands, is today consecrated

245 Booklet, 'The Abbatial Blessing of Dom Eugene Boylan', 5 August 1962. Ceremony performed by Most Rev. Joseph Rodgers, D.D., Lord Bishop of Killaloe, pp. 3–7.

abbot, being worthy of Thy sanctification, may he ever remain Thy elect, and may he never be separated from Thy grace'.

After further prayers, the bishop blesses and presents to the abbot-elect the insignia of office: the Holy Rule of St Benedict, according to which he is to govern and guard the flock entrusted to him; the Crozier of the pastoral office, which he shall bear before the flock entrusted to him, 'that while correcting vices', he may 'temper severity with charity, and when angry ... may remember mercy'; and the Ring, which is put on the abbot's finger by the bishop with the words, 'Receive this ring, the sign of faith, so that adorned with faith ... you may keep untarnished the spouse of God, the Holy Church'. After a further prayer by the bishop, this part of the ceremony concludes 'with the kiss of peace given by the bishop to the abbot'.[246]

The Mass then proceeds and continues to the final blessing. After the blessing, the bishop blesses the mitre and places it on the head of the abbot with suitable words. The abbot's gloves are likewise blessed and put on his hands. Then the bishop leads the abbot to his stall in the choir, and there delivers to him the abbot's crozier, saying, 'Receive full and free power to rule this monastery and its community, and all things known to belong to its interior and exterior government in spirituals and temporals'. After this, 'the *Te Deum* is intoned by the bishop and continued by the choir. Finally, the new abbot gives his solemn blessing to all present, and then, facing the bishop, he sings *Ad Multos Annos.'* This concludes the ceremony.[247]

Messages from Near and Far

Dom Eugene received many messages of congratulation and good wishes from his fellow Cistercians. None, perhaps, expressed better the hopes and expectations he had raised than that from Dom Columba, Abbot of Our Lady of Guadalupe Abbey, Lafayette, Oregon. On 23 July 1962, he wrote:

My dear Dom Eugene,

246 'Abbatial Blessing', pp. 10–12.
247 'Abbatial Blessing', pp. 12–15.

My sincere congratulations (and my sympathy) in that you are 'Dom' again, in a new and more important and no doubt more happy role in your own community at Roscrea. It is an extra blessing to have had the first experience at Caldey and also much spiritual contact with souls in so many other of our houses, so that you should be able to profit by your own experience and by the lessons learned from others to be a model *pastor animarum.* I presume the abbatical blessing will be expedited so that you can have things in some order before the General Chapter. My plans on this side will prevent me being in Europe 'till a few days before the Chapter, else I might make Roscrea for the occasion.

May our sweet Mother of Guadalupe have you in her keeping and grant you a long and faithful and fruitful course as abbot. *Oremus pro invicem.*[248]

Eugene's family, of course, were among those sending congratulations and prayers. There are extant letters from his sister in Glencairn and from his brother in the US, Fr Stephen, the Carthusian. Stephen offered the following advice to the new abbot:

As a vigorous new broom you will receive many suggestions as to how to sweep clean. No.1. Be lovingly severe and good-humouredly firm in the admission of novices. Only profess those who are genuine lovers of solitude and silence ... Be severe, too, for those whose family have shown a nervous or mental weakness. No.2. (A very American solution) Consider the possibility of hiring two Jesuits ... to run the college as president and vice-president, and all other teachers being laymen, and the monks having no connection with the school. No.3. Strive to avoid all distractions (hence never leave the monastery except for Chapter and unavoidable visitation). No.4. Write more books.[249]

248 External letters, File 17 (2), MSJA. *Oremus pro invicem* – let us pray for each other.
249 Stephen to Eugene, 12 July 1962, 5/5/1, MSJA. Family Correspondence.

Dom Eugene's brother in the US, Fr Stephen Boylan, a Carthusian

THE TENSIONS OF OFFICE

Of the four pieces of advice given by his brother, the evidence suggests that Eugene paid heed mainly to the last one – that he 'write more books'. The urge to write and the desire to reach out to people were powerful gifts which militated against Stephen's advice not to leave the monastery. He was 'quite convinced', he said, that 'the first and most urgent need of the moment is the extension and intensification of the interior spiritual life among all Catholics, and the application of its influence to each and every phase of their activity'.[250] He was also aware of how much he had enriched the spiritual lives of priests and religious, particularly in his emphasis on God as a God of mercy and love. In addition, the role of abbot involved him in business and social ventures, such as plans for the Mount St Joseph farm and the local farming community. Wider social and economic interests led to communication with Joe Foyle and others.

250 Interview with Matt Hoen, ed. *Catholic Authors* (1952).

Dom Columban Mulcahy, commenting on the tensions that can arise, observed that every abbot has a problem in his monastic life when he gets involved outside the monastery. Dom Eugene 'was being drawn out of the monastery to an increasing extent, but in his own spirituality he seemed very solid and well-founded'.[251] The basic principle of Eugene's spirituality, Mulcahy continued, was humility. 'He was extraordinarily humble, but at the same time very simple and naïve ... He could say the most extraordinary things about himself, but was extremely humble behind it.'[252] In this context, it is worth noting that the matter on which Eugene placed special emphasis in his talks in chapter was obedience. As we have seen, obedience had always been important for him, and he had been careful as a monk at all times to seek his superior's approval for his activities.

THE CENTRALITY OF OBEDIENCE

Within days of his elevation, Eugene spoke three times to his community on obedience. On 19 July he said that 'religious life is a life of faith ... believing that these circumstances, these superiors, these brothers will bring one to Christ and to sanctity'. Four days later he reminded the monks that 'St Benedict speaks of obedience as the way we go to God ... By obedience we don't break our wills ... we renounce them for God's will, for Christ who only is good enough for God.' After another two days he returned to the same topic: 'God is a father, an infinitely loving father, and he is father to us all day. Every religious house is ordered to let us give ourselves to God, and giving ourselves to God is a sacrifice ... Contemplation is not so much the time we spend in the chapel as in giving ourselves to God ... Contemplation can be reached in any job in the house or monastery if it is done under obedience: God will give the special graces needed.'[253]

This last point seems very important for an understanding of Eugene's spirituality. To sacrifice one's own will in obedience meant enjoying God's favour, whatever the circumstances. Thus, the free-

251 Dom Columban interviewed by Fr Nivard, MSJA.
252 Dom Columban interviewed by Fr Nivard, MSJA.
253 'Dom Eugene Chapter talks 15/7/62–1/6/1963' in 'Willie Humphries Notes', 5/5/4 ,

and-easy lifestyle he experienced in Australia, which had involved socialising, swimming and sailing, had been blessed by God because it was conducted under the umbrella of obedience as he explored the possibilities of a new foundation. It is not unlikely that Eugene, in embracing obedience, had in mind the Pauline practice of being all things to all people in order to win some for Christ (1 Cor 9:19). He felt free in the service of God, his loving father, to enjoy himself in the process.

THE PRICE OF CHANGE

Eugene knew from the narrow margin of his election victory that he was not the first choice of a considerable number of community members. He was aware that some monks feared change and that he was viewed as liberal in outlook and likely to introduce new practices. In fact, it was not just the older men who feared change and were likely to resist it. 'A strong group of younger men', too, had been opposed to his election.[254] It was characteristic of Eugene to go ahead regardless, while still regretting the lack of approval. On Holy Thursday, 11 April 1963, he referred in chapter to 'the high standard of charity in this house, and one of the things that has impressed me as abbot is the just and kind way you speak about one another with excusing mercy. I only hope that I will be spoken about in the same way.'[255]

Conscious of the criticism his absence from the monastery probably caused, he spoke in chapter on Easter Sunday, 15 April 1963, as follows: 'There is the temptation, especially for abbots, to get engrossed in the things of this world, to try and do something, to be something. We must avoid this. These things are not altogether empty. We need three meals a day. We need some notice and praise. But it is the things that are above that count. Let us pray for one another.'[256]

At the beginning of May, he returned once again to the theme of

no.3. File 7, MSJA.
254 MSJ Interviews by L. O'R, 5 June 2013, MSJA.
255 'Willie Humphries Notes', 11 April, 1963, MSJA.
256 'Willie Humphries Notes', 15 April 1963, MSJA.

obedience. 'The greater part of a monk's life is made up of trivialities, but because done by obedience they have a tremendous value. A monastery is a place where men go to God. Seeking God is all. That brings us back to the superior. God shows his will through him. An abbot will stamp his personality, even his defects, on a house. One abbot will not give enough time for study, (another will not give enough time) for choir preparation. We can see these as frustrations or we can accept them as God's will.'[257]

If any further sign were needed that Dom Eugene was not a remote intellectual but a deeply feeling human being, it was to be found in the words he spoke about the Sacred Heart, on 3 May 1963. 'We were created to be husbands and fathers, to give and receive affection, and to have families depending on us. We have a deep need for affection. It is not good for a man to be alone, but we have a helpmate like ourselves in the Word incarnate … Just as a husband is sensitive to the feelings of his wife, is faithful in small things, and lives for his family … so must our devotion be to the Sacred Heart.'[258]

Dom Eugene sought to change the spirituality of the monks. Theirs was a spirituality largely based on merit, duty and observance of the law, as was common in the Church of the time. While many people came to holiness through this spirituality, Eugene saw that it fell short of the fullness of the gospel as manifested in the New Testament and particularly in St Paul's letters. His views were strengthened by his wide reading in the history of spirituality. Accordingly, without criticising the spirituality then current, he sought to introduce a new freedom into the community, freedom in the service of a loving father, who invites us into partnership with his son, Jesus Christ.[259]

Eugene issued an invitation to the community to let go of the over-regulated regimes they had known and to embrace freely their way of life and service. The service of the Lord, he held, was to be a free action, not something mechanical. Monastic life required

257 'Willie Humphries Notes', 2 May 1963, MSJA.
258 'Willie Humphries Notes', 3 May 1963, MSJA.
259 Kinsella, *Dom Eugene Boylan*, pp. 21–2.

personal choice, he believed, and not just the following of a set of rules. This conviction led him to observe one day in chapter that 'everyone is expected to do the Office, but if you are tied up with something don't feel you are obliged'. This proved a change too far for some monks who, taking their abbot's words literally, failed to divine their true intention. Several months later, a concerned Dom Eugene is alleged to have asked, 'What am I going to do, they are not coming to the Office?'[260]

Shortly before he died, Eugene remarked to a member of the community that he was disappointed at how little impact his preaching and teaching had made on them. Undoubtedly it was naïve of him to think that a little over one year of preaching was sufficient to change a body of men of mixed background and uneven education, unused to new religious ideas. There were some, nevertheless, who were enthusiastic about their abbot's teaching and 'fervent and fully committed to change and growth'.[261]

Dom Eugene was a very different abbot from what most of the monks were used to. He was an intellectual from the city, with a reputation in 'the world' – a place which they had been accustomed to regard as alien and dangerous. Despite having a vow of stability, he was frequently absent from the monastery, which some found strange. On the other hand, they admired him as a zealous priest, a sought-after confessor and retreat director, and the author of several influential spiritual books. As if to underline his uniqueness in the community, many of his would-be critics went to him as their confessor. It is probably correct to say that many of the monks did not understand their abbot, and that he did not really understand them. The exceptions were those mentioned above, who viewed Dom Eugene as 'terrific, a breath of fresh air'.[262]

The demands and tensions of his office as abbot and his expectations of himself in that role, together with the many pressures he had experienced over years, took their toll physically and emotionally on Eugene. The official Chronicle of the abbots of

260 MSJ Interviews by L. O'R, 5 June 2013.
261 Kinsella, *Dom Eugene Boylan*, p. 21.
262 MSJ Interviews by L. O'R, 5 June 2013.

Mount St Joseph commented after Eugene's death:
> During the short period that he governed our abbey, Dom Eugene often appeared fatigued. He looked worn and more aged than he really was. The writing of books and articles, his years in the confessional, the constant calls on him as well as the austere and penitential life of the Trappist – all these, and the worries that usually accompany the lot of the superior of a large religious house, were telling their tales.[263]

THE FINAL DAYS

Despite such signs, Eugene seemed full of energy on his final day in Roscrea. The last person to speak with him before he left the monastery was Fr Nivard, who left an account of that day.[264]

> It was the day the College closed for the Christmas holidays and, as was the tradition, the parents of the boys came for the school opera. The abbot was expected to attend, make a speech, and meet parents afterwards. He had been up early that morning and had been busy all day. After the opera, he entertained a number of special guests[265] to dinner at the Guesthouse ... After the guests had departed, and we stood for a few minutes on the front steps of the Guesthouse, he told me that he was going to Sligo, which was about a three- hour drive from Roscrea. He was going to attend a funeral next day in County Donegal of the Bishop of Raphoe, William MacNeely (1923–1963). The bishop had been a priest in Derry when Eugene was a boy and had been a family friend. For 'old times sake' Eugene felt he should attend the funeral. I suggested that as he had a long day, he should go to bed and start early in the morning. He replied that

263 Claffey, 'Profiles in Sanctity', p. 33.
264 Kinsella, *Dom Eugene Boylan*, p. 20.
265 These included 'his brother, sister-in-law, and Mr Gabriel Fallon of the Abbey Theatre' according to the Quarterly of the Cistercian College, Roscrea Union, *The Roscrea Review*, No. 7, Winter 1963.

by going to Sligo he would have three quarters of the journey over, and would make it easily to the cathedral the next morning without having to start too early. I then suggested that he should have someone with him, either to drive or just to keep him awake talking. In a characteristic gesture, he put his arm around my shoulder and said, 'Don't worry about me, Son, I'll be alright'; and that was the last time I saw him alive.

On a long straight stretch beyond Roscommon town, Eugene's car left the road. It is likely that Eugene, as usual, was driving at a good speed. Perhaps there was an icy patch on the road, or perhaps he fell asleep at the wheel – we don't know, although he denied the latter suggestion. In the event, the car plunged into an adjoining field. In the sharp impact, he was thrown out through the passenger door, suffering injuries to his side. He remained semi-conscious for some time on that cold winter's night until, at some stage, a passing motorist saw the rear lights of the upended car and stopped to help.

Eugene was brought to Roscommon hospital, having suffered fractured ribs on his left side and some superficial injuries to his face and hand. He was well enough to be able to walk from the car into the hospital, but soon afterwards his condition deteriorated and for some days he was critically ill. He had contracted pneumonia and had extreme difficulty breathing.[266] According to Dom Columban, Eugene accepted his situation and, despite much pain, 'there was no complaint, no whinging'.[267]

Slowly his condition improved, and by Christmas he seemed well again. At the beginning of January 1964, he had what was thought to be a minor heart attack. A heart specialist was called and a cardiograph was taken, but the result was negative. On 5 January, Eugene seemed in excellent form and chatted with the doctors who visited him. He had received the Sacrament of the Sick – known as Extreme Unction in those days – after the heart attack, but now seemed out of danger. Then suddenly, at about 4.30 in the afternoon,

266 *The Roscrea Review*, No. 7, Winter 1963.
267 Interview with Fr Nivard previously noted.

he suffered a major heart attack. The doctors came immediately. He rallied for a few moments and then lapsed into unconsciousness. He died as his secretary, Fr Raphael, who had been staying in the hospital, was reciting the prayers for the dying.

At the post-mortem examination, it was discovered that Dom Eugene's internal injuries had been far more serious than had been realised, and that injury to his heart, as well as pneumonia, had been the cause of his death.[268] Fr Nivard, in his booklet on *Dom Eugene Boylan*, had the additional information that Eugene's accident had resulted 'in a seven-inch tear in his pericardium – the smooth membrane that surrounds the heart'.[269]

RETURN HOME AND THE OBSEQUIES

The *Roscrea Review* gave a detailed account of the removal of Eugene's remains to the Abbey in Roscrea:

> There was a large attendance as the remains were removed from the hospital to be taken back to Mount St Joseph Abbey. Included were the Bishop of Elphin, Dr Vincent Hanly, mand any priests of his diocese, members of religious orders from all over the country, past students of Roscrea College, senior Garda officers, members of the medical and legal profession, and many other sympathisers who had been coming to the hospital all day since the death was announced. Dom Camillus Claffey, Abbot Emeritus, travelled from Roscrea to bring the body back, together with a large number of mourners from the College staff and friends and neighbours of the monastery. The Midland Branch of the Past Students accompanied the funeral to Roscrea. More and more cars joined the funeral on the way down from Roscommon. Hundreds lined the street at Roscrea and the bells tolled in both Catholic and Protestant churches. A guard of honour of the farm staff accompanied the coffin as it

268 *The Roscrea Review, iam cit.*
269 Fr Nivard, op. cit., p. 20.

Dom Eugene admires Taoiseach Seán Lemass's pipe at this abbatial blessing on 5 July 1962.

entered the front gates of Mount St Joseph and proceeded to the great public church of the monastery.[270]

In the Abbey church, 'during the next two days, a constant stream of people came to pray there and to file past the coffin in which Dom Eugene's face was visible through a glass panel.'[271] Eugene's public standing was mirrored in the flood of messages of sympathy which came to the Abbey from all parts of Ireland and many parts of the world. In addition to messages from the four Catholic archbishops, from the abbots of Cistercian houses in Ireland and abroad, and from the heads of religious orders, there were messages from President Éamon de Valera, from the Taoiseach, Seán Lemass, and from James Dillon, leader of the main opposition party.

270 *The Roscrea Review* already quoted.
271 Idem.

The funeral took place after solemn requiem Mass on Wednesday, 8 January 1964. The Mass was celebrated by Bishop Rodgers of Killaloe, with Archbishop Morris of Cashel presiding. Present also were the Bishops of Limerick, Ossory and Clonfert; abbots, prelates, and up to 300 priests; representatives of the President and Taoiseach; members of the Dáil and Seanad, and former political leaders such as W.T. Cosgrave and General Richard Mulcahy. Also there to pay tribute to the late Abbot, in recognition of the new ecumenical climate, the leaders of the Protestant Churches in the locality attended the obsequies, the first time this had happened in the history of the Abbey.

TRIBUTES AND REMINISCENCES

Many tributes were paid to Dom Eugene. Few were more elaborate than the newspaper tribute from journalist, Liam Maher, who felt a personal loss at the death.

'Pope John is dead; President Kennedy is dead' – that is how millions of people all over the world will remember 1963. 'Dom Eugene Boylan is dead' – that is how I and thousands of Irish men and women will remember 1964. For us it will be a year of sadness ... for Dom Eugene was great, great in his mystical writing, his confessional genius, his penetrating preaching, his intense charity. To the Church in Ireland he brought fresh thinking, deep insight and honest appraisal ... His claim to greatness may repose most in the quiet of the confessional. Sinners he knew, understood and loved. For him sin was a symptom of an inner illness ... and he attended mental-health conferences that his confessional advice and decisions might be based on modern developments both in theology and psychology.[272]

The memory of Eugene's personal advice and teaching still lingered many years later for another journalist.

272 External Documents, 5/5/7, no. 5, MSJA. Liam Maher writing in unnamed newspaper.

When in my late teens I revolted against what I regarded as absurd Church technicalities, it was Dom Eugene Boylan, abbot of the Cistercian monastery in Roscrea when he died, who taught me to think beyond legalisms to the core of Christian beliefs. Dom Boylan was a writer and philosopher who adopted many of the views of Vatican II long before the great Pope John XXIII envisaged the holding of that council.[273]

An anonymous monk from Roscrea, who claimed to have known Dom Eugene very well and who published his reminiscences of the Abbot, claimed that Eugene had spoken to him 'many times over the years, absolutely without reserve, of his own sufferings and trials'. He revealed that Eugene 'had gone through most forms of agony a great deal more intensely than the rest of us.' Pursuing an aspect of Eugene's life so seldom mentioned, the monk remarked that 'sometimes to a person unable to look beyond his own suffering, Dom Eugene might casually mention a state of agony of soul in which he himself had been for years on end without any respite, and the self-pity of his hearer would vanish in a shameful relief at having had so little to bear by comparison'. In addition, the author declared that Eugene had often stated that he offered no new doctrine, but rather 'a new presentation of doctrine'. As regards his style of teaching, he commented that 'Dom Eugene spoke with a raw intensity. One was not conscious of receiving the official teaching of the Church, so much as a series of passionate convictions, the result of his own intense struggle to respond totally to God's love.'[274]

In an unpublished part of his manuscript, the same writer spoke of Dom Eugene's gifts as a confessor. 'He had the virtue of being a patient and peaceful listener, however rambling and incoherent the account. At the end, instantly and almost infallibly ... he would expose the real problem and offer a solution. His advice was given at once and was clear and precise... It was here that Dom Eugene

---

273 External Documents, 5/5/7 No. 5, MSJA. Fintan Tallon, 'Spirit moving people of God to renew the Church' in *Irish Times*, 27 July 1997.

274 'Remembering Abbot Boylan' by a Cistercian monk in *The Sponsor*, pp. 16–17, MSJA.

showed his greatest gift, his intuition which gave his compassion an element of empathy, by which he was able to live within another and experience his problems at first hand. And thus those in distress ... knew themselves completely understood and yet accepted and not condemned.'

Finally, in an unpublished part of his manuscript, the anonymous monk spoke of Dom Eugene in a manner that seems a fitting valediction to this gifted and unusual man and religious:

> Speaking with him I got a sense of the reality of the supernatural world. He was at home in it. With his tremendous depth and clarity and holiness he could convey that the supernatural was almost natural ... I think he had a great realisation of what was accidental to holiness. He could convey to others in simple language and concepts where holiness and the essence of religious life lay. His life and manner and whole personality certainly opened up new vistas of holiness for us. He was so different, so much himself, so unlike what you would expect of a saint, and yet you just had to recognise the holiness and sanctity of the man. Anyone who has ever met Dom Eugene cannot think that saints are blue-print, stereotyped, carbon-copy figures. I thank God for the grace of having known him.[275]

---

275 'Dom Eugene', Grey Box 11, MSJA. No author named, but is the same anonymous 'Cistercian Monk' who wrote in *The Sponsor.*

CHAPTER 13

An Enduring Legacy

Eugene Boylan's distinctive family life enabled him to become self-confident, at ease in society, ambitious and committed to hard work. These features were accompanied by a restless energy which, in his sister's words, rendered him 'fidgety'. It was noted early on that he was reserved in his relationships, but also that people sometimes came to him with problems and that he gave them his full attention. The regime of trust he experienced at home, together with his fairly independent life at school in Dublin, left him resentful of the conformity and regulations imposed by seminary life.

At university, something of his mother's flamboyance revealed itself in his involvement in a variety of societies, and in particular in his prominence as debater, and later as auditor, in the Literary and Historical Society in UCD. Despite his social involvements, he worked hard and won a physics scholarship to the University of Vienna. There, he led a life that he looked back on as 'halcyon'. Nevertheless, both in Dublin and in Vienna, he reflected on his religious beliefs, thought them through, and was comfortable in defending them. At some stage in those years, or shortly afterwards, he came across Paul De Jaegher's *One with Christ*, which opened his eyes and changed the course of his spiritual life.

He felt a call to religious life and chose a monastic order, a choice that we can now see was consonant with his previous life. To his peers at school he had been popular but 'different'. The option for monastic life was also 'different'. He liked the public scene and enjoyed being centre-stage, but there was something about him that was apart from others and self-reliant. He brought to monastic life the spirit of hard work that had proved successful in his studies, and he remained outwardly very much himself.

He was something of a novelty in cloistered life at the time. With his academic reputation, his city background, his Viennese experience and his friendly, assured manner, he introduced colour and the whiff of a wider world into the circumscribed lives of men who were mostly from a rural background and a society that had basically remained unchanged despite political upheavals and different allegiances. His earnest embrace of monastic life, his singing and musical ability in choir, his genuine interest in the Cistercian tradition, and his clear desire to follow the path to holiness won over any of those who were initial hostile to this new and 'different' member of the community.

Subsequently, his difference from others was accentuated by his books and their success, the publicity these generated, and his absence from time to time to give retreats and conferences. On the other hand, he was at one with the others in his devout celebration of the Mass, his active participation in the Divine Office, his deep devotion to Our Lady as Mother of the Mystical Body of Christ, and his great reputation as a confessor and spiritual guide. The tension between the required stability of monastic life and his activity outside the monastery was to be a feature throughout Eugene's monastic career.

What distinguished him for people in the wider world were the depth of his writings and the compelling conviction of his conferences. In both areas he displayed a capacity to adapt his message to his audience, and to render 'the supernatural almost natural'. Through it all, and helping to carry it all, was a combination of ambition and driving energy. At a personal level, he had an easy charm of manner, while revealing little of himself. To the end of his life he retained a sort of boyishness which found expression in his delight in fast cars, his visits to familiar laboratories in his former university, and the fondness in which he held his recollections of Vienna. There he had experienced the melody of life, and he never forgot it.

It is surely significant that what received most attention at the time of his death were his patience, insight and compassion as a confessor. In an era of frequent confession, he spent hours on end listening to people's concerns and relieving many of them of heavy burdens. He introduced numerous men, women and children to a

God of love and understanding, in place of the God of obligation and judgement to which they were accustomed.

In his monastic life he grew spiritually over the years, travelling a long and sometimes painful road. His early enthusiasm and consolation in prayer were followed by a time of failure and discouragement as a teacher. Distaste for prayer and a seeming absence of God followed, and later his rejection at Caldey was added to his pain. Finally, back in Roscrea, he moved closer to the ideal which he espoused all his life, of emptying himself for Christ. At this point, his reputation as an author seemed of little importance to him, and he probably resonated with the insight that led St Thomas

Aquinas to declare that all of his monumental work was mere straw. What was important was 'to put on Christ' *(Gal 3:27)*. Eugene was now closer to reaching the desired goal he had set himself much earlier when he wrote to his sister in the Cistercian monastery at Glencairn, 'There's no meaning in being a Cistercian unless we see it as a means of giving ourselves to Him and replacing ourselves by Him'.

As abbot, Eugene's restless mind and body found the day-to-day trivia of his job tiresome, and he sought outlets from the work of administration. In that respect he was not an effective abbot. He sought to renew the spiritual outlook of his monks, but felt he had failed. Yet, as one of his admirers observed, 'his legacy endures in a Christ-centred spirituality, in freedom of spirit, and in his approach to the life of prayer. He saw these as central not only to the life of the monk but to anyone seeking God.'

Eugene died at sixty years of age, seemingly before his time. As to his inner thoughts during his final days, one can only speculate. All those who knew him had no doubt that he was at peace to the end, open to whatever might arise as part of God's plan. This was only to be expected of the one who had taught all his life about confidence in God and acceptance of God's will. 'The whole of God's will has only one purpose,' he had written in *This Tremendous Lover*, 'to re-establish everything in Christ. Therefore, if our wills are conformed to the will of God, the whole of our history ... is part of a plan ... to unite us to Christ and sanctify us in him.'[276]

276 Kinsella, *Dom Eugene Boylan*, p. 24.

INDEX